From Maryland to

Alaska and Back

A Promise Fulfilled

By

Scott Price

From Maryland to Alaska and Back: A Promise Fulfilled
by Scott A. Price

For additional information, book orders, & press materials, please visit:
http://www.CelebrateBig.com/promise

Published from Seattle, Washington
Printed in the United States of America
Celebrate Big Publishing

Library of Congress Control Number: 2009900930

ISBN 978-0-578-00984-1

Dedicated to my Parents

The fuel for this journey

Contents

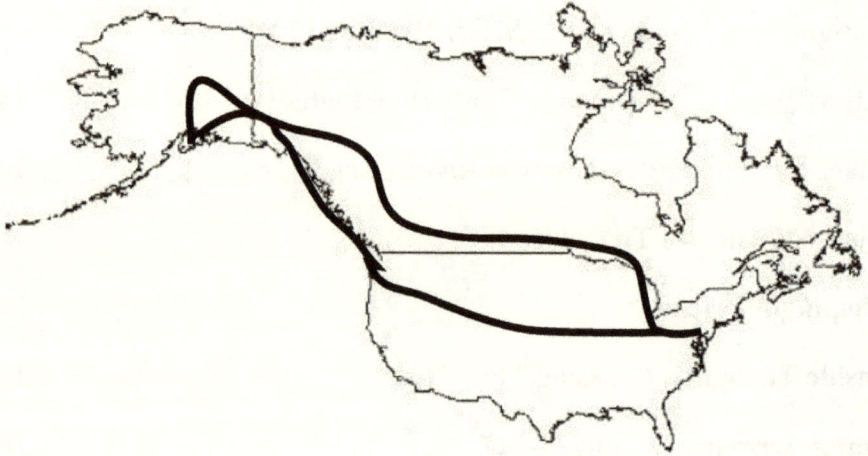

PROLOGUE

The whole mobile shindig began ten years before, when Dad bought the same Suzuki that I later rode to Alaska. We were on our first motorcycle camping trip together. Dad started his mental gears meshing and rolling when he saw my early interest in motorcycles at the age of twelve, and he was thinking ahead. A future journey was born.

Neither of my parents had the opportunity to go to college, and it was very important to them that both my brother and I had that opportunity. While Dad and I sat around a crackling campfire, poking at the coals, he said we would go on a motorcycle trip to Alaska together if I graduated from college. That seemed cool to a budding teenager, but it was a long way off. But I finally did receive that piece of paper proclaiming my graduation in 1989, and Dad was true to his word as always.

For me, the real planning and contemplating began two years before this trip. I had essentially forgotten about the whole promise while still a teenager, but sophomore year of college Dad nonchalantly reminded me that I needed to get a motorcycle license so I could start practicing well in advance of our long journey. He was actually getting serious about this stuff… So we started making some vague plans. Specific itineraries were too restrictive. The trip became an ongoing source of conversation and a filter for what we read.

He started teaching me how to ride a motorcycle. No complaints there. I did not need a reason to hop on a motorcycle; having a larger goal just made it better. Besides, this was a "good solid reason" that would pass Mom's approval test.

As June came near, our local newspaper The Aegis had a big spread about us. They loved the concept of the very long distance father and son trip, and they really liked something unusual to splash ink onto their newsprint. So right after hauling all my college stuff back from Tufts, we met a reporter at Dad's place of work. The rain was heavy and I arrived for the interview wet in a couple embarrassing spots. Some of my leather even shrunk. Upon our return from this journey, we had another big story in the newspaper summarizing our tale for the locals, which sparked another wave of interest from everyone around.

Dad was well-wished by many people that he saw prior to rolling away from our little town of Jarrettsville, and we attained a small level of local notoriety after that Aegis article hit the stands. One of my high school teachers gave me a call to wish me well, as well as friends I had not heard from in a long while. I even talked to the owner of our local garbage disposal company over the phone; I had no idea who he was but he was very enthusiastic since he had been on long motorcycle trips himself. Many relatives and friends wished us well and, of course, told us to drive safe...

The journey ahead was set to open my eyes to the possibilities of the world. Its beauty, its people, its possibilities, its hidden nooks and open expanses. And it served as a "can do" bridge to life beyond home and college. This was all very possible, very real, and about to begin.

ON THE ROAD: MARYLAND TO OHIO

Day 1: 319 miles this day / 319 miles total so far

It was creeping up to 1 a.m. the night before, and we still had more packing to do. So, we procrastinated and went to sleep, waking up that first morning to the sound of pounding rain with thunder. We packed clothes, camping gear, and a Frisbee into separate sets of a tank bag, two saddle bags, and a large duffel bag, plus little things jammed here and there in the few extra nooks and crannies that a motorcycle offered. We made everything semi-water-resistant with plastic bags, covers, and wrapped-around tarps. Personal water resistance was provided by bright yellow rubber ducky suits.

As we pulled around the front of the house with family cameras on us and people waving goodbye, Dad's BMW stalled and would not restart. It could be kick started, but the electric starter was just taking up extra weight.

Dad had a sick feeling and cursed his luck. After all of his hard work in preparing for this trip, his initial moment was snatched. Back to the garage.

We went over the electrical spaghetti and found that the starter relay switch was all screwed up. We tried to cannibalize from a friend's Beemer, but the bikes had different visions of what a starter system should have been. Dad eventually disassembled the relay thingy and fixed it with a squeeze of his pliers. The long delay kept us at home for a couple more hours, but it offered up a rain-free and only partly-cloudy afternoon. Off came the rubber ducky suits. No complaints again.

We zoomed off with a wave and rev of the engines, aiming at Pennsylvania on highway 83 and crossing west on the Pennsylvania Turnpike to eventually end up a little way down the Ohio Turnpike at the Ohio Motel in North Lima.

The interstate riding was a surprisingly good time. The traffic was sparse and easy to maneuver through. The setting was the best part, though. Rural areas looked like real life saturated Fuji color film, and my pinkish/brownish/greenish sunglasses (custom colored by me) gave the view a Norman Rockwell look on hallucinogens. Greens stuck out brightly, shadows deepened to black. Passing in and out of shadow acted as a strobe light, and the interesting mountain clouds stood well defined against the deepened blue behind them. Curves of sloping hills lined with meandering forests - cut through by our highway - was quite the visual game.

The strangest thing of the day, though, was attempting to get accustomed to wearing our between-helmet radio walkie talkies. Dad and I spent more time testing the system and asking each other "can you hear me now?" than actually conversing about what we were seeing. I sometimes felt obliged to say something just to be polite, and the silent non-talking time - natural to a motorcycle - was now weird. The contraption violated my personal thoughts and privacy usually provided by wind buffeted solo anonymity. I eventually became somewhat accustomed and let it recede from my thoughts, but it was still lurking.

That first night, Dad snored away in his bed as I wrote. Mom said he tended to snore more when tired, and long days on a motorcycle immediately popped to mind as something that might be filed in the "tiring" manila folder. He got about an hour's head start on my sleep, and I hadn't even showered yet, so I could see that book writing was going to take a toll on my sleep hours...

ADJUSTING AND SEEING: INTO CANADA

Day 2: 573 / 892

That first night's sleep situation was not as bad as predicted, though an extra hour would have been real nice. Dad woke me by walking around the room loudly and announcing the day with a very bright light. "Yeah yeah yeah I'm coming" was the thought of the moment, though my squinty eyes, gravelly voice, and lack of movement was saying otherwise. However I was also ready to get some miles done, so up and out I went.

We headed along the Ohio Turnpike, with clear cool weather and a half moon floating to our left even into the afternoon. Being good Americans, we stopped at McDonald's for breakfast. I greased up and weighted down, and we were off and cruising again.

My funkadelic shades proved to be even more valuable than they were the day before. They created a new vision of everything that we were passing through. It was amazing how much a "normal, everyday" scene could be transformed by peering through these prescription portholes. The details and shades across clouds were so much more pronounced. I always knew my glasses made the greens of trees and plants more vibrant, but this day I took that a step further and realized something more important. The glasses differentiated greens of different types of trees, giving each a different tone and intensity. Otherwise bland, monochromatic scenes took on depth and nuanced visual interest. The glasses did tend to make the world very dark and contrasty when looking in the direction of the sun. In other words, they were not very effective as... sunglasses. But that created a character all its own. I was just required to be more vigilant and hoped that nothing would jump out at me from the murky shadows.

With regard to the technological contraptions dangling inside, outside, and below our helmets, things were improving. Their intrusion on my motorcycle personal space was still there and forced my thoughts on occasion, but they were gradually fading away into being just another piece of equipment. The miles and solitude rolled on.

The Ohio landscape immediately impressed me with its flatness. This - combined with the lack of trees that were long ago subjugated by farm land - allowed for a deep view away from the road to each side. For some unknown reason, I noticed many more plumes of rising smoke than I had ever seen in other states, except perhaps for rotten egg smelling industrial areas. I knew some were from smokestacks, but I could not see the source of most. Perhaps the flatland's lack of obstructions granted a view that would have been similarly seen in other states had they also been clear cut and scraped down to dirt everywhere.

The farm land was interesting, especially with the view through my super-shades. Rotting barns reflected off of small ponds, followed by rows of trailer homes as counterpoint. There was even a fading painting of a Middle Eastern guy, with beard and turban, filling up the entire front of an old red barn. I'd like to have known the story on that one.

Around about Toledo we headed up route 23, which eventually merged with 75. The highway became progressively more pleasant and remote as we travelled north. In the initial areas of heavier traffic, Dad brought up a great point: he asked if I had come to any conclusions about the cars in the area. Having not even given it any thought, I responded "no".

"Count the number of foreign cars that you see."

Ah. It was unique, from my experience, to see a parade of 99.9% GM, Ford, and Chrysler products flowing the other way. We were entering Detroit country. A union billboard flashed by, instructing us to buy American. We rumbled by on our Suzuki and BMW.

Further up the road and out beyond the hubbub, we cranked out some relaxed miles cruising at around 75 miles per hour. An occasional switch of lanes to pass or be passed broke the rhythm. The warmth of my "poopysuit" - the name given by Dad to our black cold weather riding outfits - mixed together with the wind buffeting, the droning sounds of rushing air, and the spinning engine to lull me for a while. I finally nodded off and the ensuing spurt of adrenaline from the "stay alive" section of my brain did a good job at keeping me conscious for the rest of the day.

The road became very remote, at least in appearance, blocked off from the rest of the world by thick trees on both sides of our two lanes. Even the oncoming lanes were separated by trees and usually out of sight. It was a great stretch of road to rack up miles, flowing forward on the tarmac.

People's reactions to our motorcycles and to us were always amusing. The combination of our spaceman suits with reflective orange safety vests, heavily laden motorcycles, and signs on each motorcycle telling the world "Alaska or Bust" received so many different reactions. On the road, we got stares, laughs, look-aways, pointed fingers, and thumb-ups. When we stopped somewhere for a rest, gas, or food, a wide range of unique people would initiate a conversation from out of nowhere. These were people we would otherwise have never met if we were in a car and looked normal.

The cashier at a Marathon gas station mothered us and told us our snacks were not nutritious enough, while a friendly man with his family kept elaborating on his trips to Europe. The family life had strapped him down, so he had not taken any extended trips in the prior few years. I wondered why that procreation business was so popular.

We ended the day crossing the border into Canada. It was an interesting change. The obvious differences centered around leaving a bunch of American trees and coming over a high bridge into the Canadian lights of Sault Ste. Marie. Suddenly, we were surrounded by canals and a customs inspection station which I suppose served some sort of purpose for some sort of reason.

The customs practices were so lax between the two countries that I could have easily brought in a bazooka stuffed with cocaine. The more subtle changes caught my attention, though. All of the businesses were different, though the movies were all American. That was interesting in itself, but the choices of store names, items on sale, advertising, and services were all unique to Canada. Even the stop lights, the curve of the intersections, and the shape of direction arrows painted on the road were different.

Dad got a sleeping jump ahead of me again that evening. He wrote a cursory journal entry, and headed off to sleep quickly. No problem with that; just have mercy on my gravelly voiced body the next morning…

MOSQUITOES AND THE OLD WOMAN: TRANS-CANADIAN HIGHWAY

Day 3: 453 / 1345

D ad slept in more than I thought, gradually getting away from his pre-trip norm of long hours at work to put me through college, pay too many bills, and then gallivant off to a month-long trip to Alaska. He had to continue to suck it in and push onward for years, but he did so and as always certainly earned more of my respect in the process, just as my mother had earned doing the same. Now he was relaxing a bit.

We began our Canadian experience by Windexing away the swarms of American bugs that became permanently elongated on our windscreens and helmets. I noticed they were building up a fairly thick solid layer behind the rearview mirrors, and the bugs were starting to make a strong showing on the shin area of my pants and poopysuit. We were rolling bug death machines.

Mosquitoes started to form swarms around us for the first time too. We must have officially arrived up north, since it was infamous for this. Once I put on my helmet, my sealed spacesuit was complete and I didn't care if there were swarms of pterodactyls around my head. I knew that I confused some of them when I would remove my helmet. They would follow my beheaded "head" to wherever I set the helmet down, finally recognizing the meager nutritional value of fiberglass and coming back for the rest of me.

While I was suited up in my armor and waiting for Dad to come out of the bank where he was exchanging American paper for the more colorful Canadian variety, a woman appeared and gave some local insight. She recommended that we delete the "t" from our "Alaska or Bust" sign. Now that's a thinking lady.

After a few miles into the meat of the Trans-Canadian Highway and a few miles out of Sault Ste. Marie, I realized that this Canada stuff was getting real interesting real quick. The scenery/sights along the road were amazing. It was nature's natural, not a park-like natural. The dense, lush trees were so many different shades of green that they reminded me of the sunglasses-effect, without the assist of the sunglasses. There was a full range from the bright light greens of the aspens (with their contrasting white bark) to the dark varieties of conifers. Leaning through long sweeping turns created the effect of moving through a huge bowl of trees. They rose on both sides and around the curves, forming their own reality.

Every once in a while I would arbitrarily look 90 degrees to my side, directly into the forest. It was incredible the number of times that I would suddenly see a body of water. Canada was waterlogged. If someone looked at a map of the area, it would seem that a boat would be more valuable than a motorcycle.

Our entire trip today circumvented the north shores of Lake Superior. The lake was humongous. After all of the miles put behind us that day, we were still a big jump away from leaving it behind. And the lake was a popular bowl for beautiful cascading rivers to flow into. The rivers always splashed with drama over rocks, making a great series of rapids or drop-off waterfalls.

I frequently got the urge to stop and appreciate, but We Must Push On. If we dilly-dallied there, then we may have been forced to grudgingly pass by our goal locations in Alaska and the Northwest. And that would have been a sad no-no. However, the Trans-Canadian Highway held many opportunities for another trip, and a relaxed pace with a camera along would be very welcome.

We eventually stopped at Old Woman Bay. Unfortunately the Old Woman was not very kind to me. She must not have liked motorcyclists. She first convinced the overhanging gray clouds to let loose with some drizzle. Being the mentally and physically prepared travelers that we were, we started unloading and fumbling with multiple layers of weather protection that we had to cover all of our baggage and every square inch of ourselves. Considering how multiple these layers really were, it was taking so long to condom over the motorcycle that I was getting mildly irritated. I hate boring, repetitive tasks. The Old Woman thought that she would scold me for my lack of patience by having my shiny helmet slip off of the handlebars. It appropriately bounced around on the asphalt for a while, shedding some useless chips of paint from various spots on its previously like-new surface, and rolled into the sand trap (beach). Fine, then I did not have to worry over its pristine veneer anymore. Thanks, Old Woman. I suppose that she got really mad at my mild acceptance of the mild punishment, so she decided to sock me with a doozy.

After Dad had taken off and gone out to the road, I tried to make a sharp half-circle turn in the parking lot. Of course the bike balked and broncoed some, steering me just off course enough to put me in the sand. I found that directional control of 700 pounds of Suzuki decreased significantly in the sand, especially when performing a slow turn. So, of course, I laid the bike down for a rest. I had been devirginated from not having dropped a motorcycle. I suppose I should have been happy to have completed this rite of passage.

That evening we ended up in Thunder Bay at the Sleeping Giant Motor Hotel. I probably should have refused to stay here just because of the corny hotel name, but the beds were rectangular and the soap lathered. No complaints.

TRANSITIONS: TO BRANDON, MANITOBA

Day 4: 596 / 1941

D ad's natural wakeup call came a little too early this morning for my comfort, but we did want to get moving for some accumulated miles. To help us get out on the road fairly quickly, we did the bulk of our motorcycling duties the prior night. Dad also concocted a gizmo on my throttle grip such that a small bracket protruded out perpendicular to the handlebar. I was having trouble with my throttle hand: a lack of circulation due to the hard grip needed and the high frequency vibration from the engine, compounded with many hours of many miles. The bracket and clamp acted as a hand rest, allowing me to palm the throttle open instead of constantly squeezing it. This day's 596 mile test session had marked improvement in all quantifiable aspects of hand performance. Experimental methods soon to be published.

The poopysuits earned their share of baggage space that morning as well. The weather was clear and very cool, with layer over layer of wispy clouds stretching in upward directions. It warmed nicely during the day, though. After a slow ride through gravel road construction areas (with not much cooling air swishing over me), I peeled off the poopysuit and replaced it with a black leather jacket at the next gas stop. I paused in between to drink a refreshing root beer and let some of my ski-suit-induced sweat evaporate away.

Wispy clouds bulked up during the course of the day; most of the late afternoon and evening became overcast. The cloud designs were great to see, especially when I still had my shades on as a left-over from when it was sunny. Light streaks filtered through to the ground from time to time, and layers of clouds created the wispy patterns over top of diffused oil paint shapes, all with an occasional dash of watercolor stains on paper. It was elongated chromatography in the sky.

We rolled through many landscape transitions. The early going was similar to the day before, but I became somewhat desensitized to it all because of input overload. I was getting mildly complacent about the beauty, probably just like the locals who drove through every day.

It was becoming normal. The number and proportion of coniferous trees gradually increased, reaching 100% for one stretch of road that made me feel as if I was washing down a trough lined by pines. The trees were periodically being hacked down in rectangular sections for timber or pulp, though. Somewhat jarring.

The land flattened considerably to the point where an occasional rise would attract my geologic attention. This increasing flatness eventually served a purpose for Canadian homo sapiens: farmland. The horizons suddenly opened up about forty miles before Winnipeg. Somewhat jarring again, but the openness and flat, straight roads were a productive change of pace for our mileage-busting cruising.

Other areas were much more visually and aesthetically interesting, but this provided a glimpse of Canadian-style farming. I could see far enough in one direction that floating mirages appeared over the horizon beyond the fields. Coming up on Winnipeg was also a strange sensation. Seeing a city of skyscrapers out way beyond the fields, in the middle of wherever-that-was, rising up after hundreds of open miles on miles, was surreal. We circumvented the city and continued rolling down the Trans-Canadian, which had changed route numbers from 17 to 100 to 1 over its course. The land transformed into a topographer's nightmare: groups of small, rolling hills all oddly shaped and tightly packed together. The trees were sparse and short; bushes and grasses had the upper hand.

I continued to be impressed by the pleasant people we met. I talked a while to a backpack- and guitar-laden hitchhiker who was European in origin but lived and worked in Toronto. He had travelled in a friend's car to Banff and was hitching back, mostly with truckers. No room for him on our bikes. Dad also struck up a conversation with the proprietor of an Esso gas station. We had just ridden 208 miles non-stop and our numbed butts were ready to do some hanging out. Both the proprietor and her huge St. Bernard gave us their full attention.

We ended up at The Little Chalet in Brandon, Manitoba. I had never been in a real honest-to-goodness prefab chalet before. It even included color TV and a wavy bathroom floor (from water rotting it). It was quiet and comfortable, and simple. The shower was a bit cramped and I had not tried the bed yet, but a table was performing very well as a hard writing surface. The plan for the next day: count up a bunch more scenic miles, possibly to Calgary.

Did you hear that, butt? Enjoy the chalet while you can. Vibration awaited in the morning.

WIDE OPEN: BIG CANADA TO CALGARY

Day 5: 707 / 2648

I was writing in the lobby of our new temporary shelter (the Pointe Inn) this evening, but the vibes were not right. The only place to write was on a tabletop videogame which had pixelated and pixilated ninjas beating people up, and the lighting was rather dim. I could have handled the violent virtual warriors dancing around behind my book, but my eyes were rather tired. Too much time looking at the world through glasses and too much wind blast around those facechangers.

That wind blast seeping into my helmet indirectly put me into somewhat of a pissy mood. We had been riding for many nonstop miles when my right eye started hurting big time and then became welded shut with tears rolling out. I first got irritated for no rational reason because I was trying to dodge one-eyed through traffic to catch up to Dad and tell him to pull over. The presence of traffic in this traffic-less country was an "it figures" situation.

After finally stopping Dad, my eye hurt even more when trying to re-open it. Then my mild form of a bad mood was cemented into place when an eighteen wheeler whizzed by our motorcycles on side stands, pushing a gust of wind our way that literally lifted my helmet into the air and bounced it down the highway. I sat brooding while my eye slowly recovered from the drying wind.

Canada again flaunted how big it was, but we got in our longest chunk yet. The aftermath: I was slightly lightheaded from vibrating bones, constricting helmet, and too much noise since I had not worn my ear plugs this day. The ride was still very loud even when I had the little yellow foam puff balls in place, but always a lot louder without them. At night in bed, Dad shut his eyes and – absolutely no exaggeration – he was lightly snoring in about twenty seconds. Quickest sleeper this side of Lake Superior. Instead of taking our usual 100 mile rest stops, we generally kept going this day until around 150 miles and then we would fill up the motorcycle tanks with machine food.

Since we were in eat-up-the-pavement mode, our speeds were up to about 80 miles per hour. Each day had been faster than the one before. The usual top speeds that we hovered around were 60 on

Saturday, 65 on Sunday, 70 on Monday, 75 on Tuesday, and 80 this day. I sensed a pattern. We would be going over 200 mph by the end of the trip.

The morning began where we were before: Canadian farmland. The terrain was much drier than other areas from the past few days, but some recent rain livened it up. I was most impressed by the variety of birds. They were easy to spot since they were always out in the open on directly visible spots such as the ground, telephone wires, or sign posts. There was not much else for them to choose from when flying near a highway in the middle of farmed-over flatland. The birds ranged from a bright yellow chested black bodied bird to an eagle to little birds that flitted up and down like butterflies.

Farmland eventually changed to low rolling mounds ("hills" was too big a word) of healthy green pasture. Although the rises were very low, they formed a complete bowl-like horizon around myself when I rode through the troughs. I could not see beyond the rim because everything beyond was low as well. The highway was traced at a distance by who-knows-how-long barbed wire fence, telephone wires on poles, and train tracks that I saw put to use on many more occasions than I ever saw at home in the red white and blue. With the exception of several wild pronghorn antelope and motorists, the only other animals were cattle. They were in bunches or alone, all standing, walking, or lying down. I saw that all they really did was masticate, stare intently at some things as if they were important, look unfocused at other things lazily, and grow tender or manufacture milk. And they probably did not have the brains to know how boring their lives were.

I also noticed three things Canadians seemed to love:

1. Semicircular Quonset huts. They were most popular on farms, but were also used for storage, stores, and garages. Roof varieties ranged from shingles to corrugated steel.

2. Fancy intersections in the boondocks. Every so often I came upon an intersection that looked as though it was lifted out of Los Angeles, but the only thing around would be perhaps a mill (very popular also) or a smoke plume in the distance that was perhaps from some surface mining / digging equipment. The intersections were complete with bypass bridges and jug handle exit ramps, but there were never any cars bypassing or exiting, and the vacant intersecting roads just went off into the open distance. I supposed the Canadians subscribed to a "too much is better than too little" philosophy, or else there was some pork barrel government funding being spread around.

3. Waterslides. These things were all over. I even saw a billboard advertisement claiming that a motel had one. It must have been a national sport or something.

Alberta had a sign fetish, too. As soon as I crossed the line into the province, I was inundated with sign after sign after sign. All were pleasant and kept me awake (maybe their intention), but some were amazingly superfluous.

One of my favorite signs was actually before all of this in the pasture land of Manitoba. A large, official-brown sign announced the name of the area we were entering in big bold letters. Below that it stated "Entering Tourist Zone". I looked in every direction to the horizon and could not even find a masticating cow, let alone a Tourist Zone.

Another favorite sign, which was used frequently in sign-happy Alberta, announced in yellow: "Important Intersection Ahead". The Important Intersection usually involved a one-lane gravel road coming onto the highway, all the way from over the distant horizon, and with no vehicles anywhere to be seen. And that was it. Uh huh.

We were in Calgary this evening and saw the mountains below red backlit blue-gray clouds with yellow-orange wisps further out. I saw the mountains about fifty miles of traveling before Dad did, but I first mistook them as oddly shaped and colored clouds which fascinated me by how much they resembled mountains. Dad pointed the *mountains* out when he noticed them, and I learned a lesson in perceived perception.

INTO THE MOUNTAINS: ROCKIES, BANFF, AND JASPER

Day 6: 235 / 2883

T he amount of summer daylight in the northern latitudes was great for traveling and setting up a camp in the evening, though synchronizing to the time of day was somewhat disorienting for us southerners. Watches had no place of consequence on a trip like this, but they were a subtle reminder of how soon the sun would be floating up again. Unless the window shades were drawn tight, light from outside easily woke me up. In a tent, there were no shades and sunlight filtered through the breathable fabric. So the situation was worse there. But sleeping in a tent had the advantage of feeling fresh, unlike a musty motel room with asylum white cinder block walls. So it was all about making compromises wherever we rested.

After leaving Calgary we went searching in nearby Cochrane for a BMW motorcycle dealer, which was *very* difficult to find anywhere in Canada, let alone on this side of the country. Eventually we found one, and I thought Dad had found his Motorcycle Heaven: Motospezial. He loved the place, and said later he almost would have liked to stay longer than we did. No dealership ever quite turned me on, but I did agree that Cochrane, Alberta had the best motorcycle dealership I had ever seen. The parts selection was good though nothing overly abundant, but they had a full range of every two-wheeled BMW available on the well-kept showroom floor and the people were very pleasant. Motospezial was owned by a husband and wife, with him coming from England and having spent a lot of time in Germany, and her from Germany (and, by default, having spent a lot of time in Germany...).

Dad needed a new side mirror since the BMW had vibrated off its center-stand and tipped over in front of our rented prefab chalet, breaking off the mirror. They had one. He also considered getting the starter relay switch that had screwed him over on the first day of this trip. And he also wanted new mufflers since the loud aftermarket boomers were rattling his brain coils. The husband - who ran most of the show - exchanged a used set of two-into-one mufflers for Dad's set-of-two plus $100 Canadian. Everybody was happy when all was done.

We pointed our bikes toward the looming Canadian Rockies and whizzed through a landscape of growing hills. Mounds turned into foothills, and we eventually wound through valleys, mountains, and a large Native Indian population on to Banff National Park. Wow! It was a place that spoke for itself, but I will translate a little anyhow.

Riding through Banff National Park

First impressions came through dense forests of conifers rising steeper and steeper to the treeline, above which laid barren rock twisted and folded into curved strata. The mountains were topped with windblown snow, and that vista especially appealed to Dad. Wildlife seemed to love its relative safety in this artificially bounded natural home. There were many deer, bighorn sheep, and a black, blue, and white bird that was quite possibly the most beautiful bird I had ever seen.

Our first walk-around, get-off-the-bikes place was Lake Louise. Very pretty, but the huge hotel on its shore and the postcardy feel (that said a million people have already taken that same photograph I just did) diminished the effect for me. Waterfowl Lake was actually much more to my liking. Lots of bugs, no tour busses, no people, serene, and wonderful in its own right. I was glad there was no overlook. The overlook-mentality - "let's stop here because there is a place to pull off; if there is no pull-off then it must not be worth looking at" - did not work well with me. That is not to imply that there was no pull-off for Waterfowl Lake, because there was one. But a short hike removed me from the road and put me on a rock by the lapping water. Granted it was a self-delineated distinction, but important nonetheless.

Lake Louise in Banff

Waterfowl Lake in Banff

As the sun arced low in the valley, we continued heading north and came upon something truly impressive: the Weeping Wall. Depending upon how one counted, there were sixteen distinct waterfalls tumbling over a high cliff. In one instance, a waterfall broke over a ledge into two waterfalls. And my personal favorite was one waterfall which evenly divided itself into four equally spaced waterfalls. I was briefly tempted to take a picture, but realized that a quick photograph seemed to only belittle the true experience when actually present.

We ended our late evening with a walk onto Athabasca Glacier in Jasper National Park. It felt like a large pile of snow to me, but conceptualizing the forces and magnitudes involved gave all glaciers a special interest. Some glaciers we saw were very slowly cascading down the steep sides of mountains, impressive in their form, looking much like the frozen rivers of snow and ice that they were.

We rolled on through the Jasper twilight and parked for the evening at Jonas Creek campground. After schlepping our baggage up flights of wooden stairs and into our woody campsite, we ate a good camp dinner of hot Mini Raviolis and canned fruit cocktail. My head got cold during the night, lacking the protection of the sleeping bag, but I slept well even if not for long.

WATER FLOWING: JASPER

Day 7: 219 / 3102

Jasper was our turf today, and it continued to outdo itself like Banff had done the day before. The mountains rose up smoothly on both sides: God's halfpipe. The wildlife was even better than we saw in Banff. The number was not as large, but the pickings were great. Later in the day we saw two black bears eating plants and also were stared at by a curious coyote.

Most of our stops centered around waterfalls. I wrote postcards to friends above the roaring power of Sunwapta Falls, wanting to share the moment with them. Athabasca Falls was at least as impressive, flowing from a rushing river onto rocks well below the footpath bridge. Following the water's path was aesthetically interesting since the years of flowing erosion left smooth-sculpted rock chambers and curves.

Sunwapta Falls in Jasper National Park

Those falls were somewhat dwarfed by the dimensions and shapes of Maligne Canyon. The canyon was a thin slit in the Earth (23 feet across), yet disproportionately deep (167 feet at its deepest). A huge waterfall cut into its beginning rim and fell unimpeded into a dark, swirling lagoon below. The cascading river traveled further through the canyon walls until it all eventually broke out into a valley. One of a kind and completely unexpected.

Dad and I decided to head over to Medicine Lake and Maligne Lake before turning around and heading west out of the park. We enjoyed the winding roads as much as seeing the lakes, and the combination felt good. The Log-Tel Hotel kept us comfortable after travelling through Mount Robson Provincial Park and some road construction zones to McBride.

The signs that warned "Extreme Dust Hazard: Use Headlights" were not kidding. In fact, the construction workers let us travel ahead of the "pilot vehicle" construction truck that led everyone through at a slow pace. They realized our relative nakedness and let us go ahead of the suspended dust storm that billowed from the moving line of vehicles behind us.

Looking down into Maligne Canyon

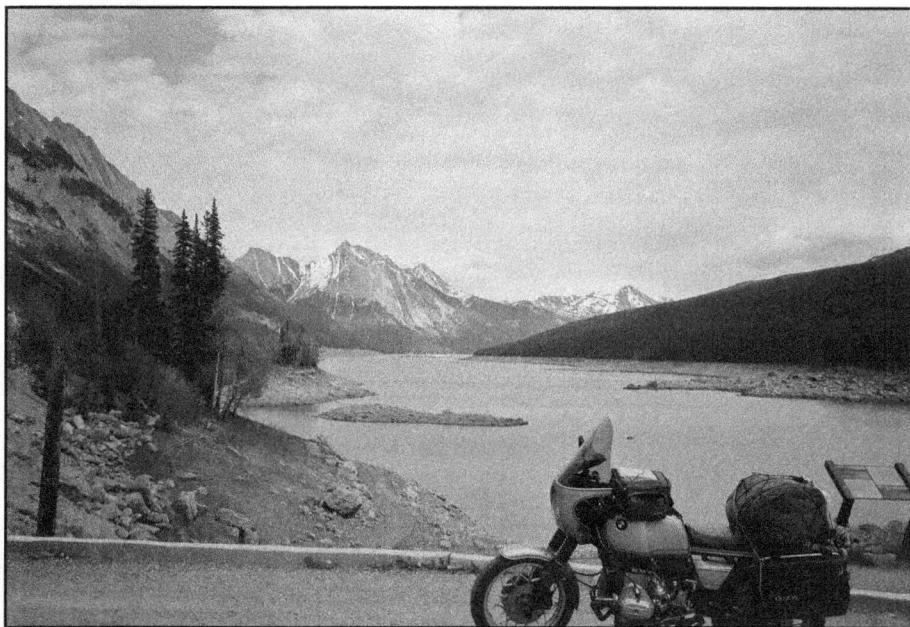

Medicine Lake in Jasper

THE CURVE OF THE ROAD: TO DAWSON CREEK

Day 8: 437 / 3539

Today was a quality day for simply enjoying the roads. We headed out of McBride and into the mountains, which reversed their earlier growth and shrunk to conifer-covered hills, eventually ending in smooth, rolling mounds of pasture land and farmland near Dawson Creek. I enjoyed leaning the Suzuki back and forth through the tree-lined curves, each one a little different than all the others. Bridges overlooked river-bottom gorges and changed the scenery, but most of my attention was on the road and the bike. I let my thoughts fly around, and they touched on everything from my future motorcycle racing plans, to my new post-college job that I was going to start shortly after this trip, to grappling with the roots of past arguments I had with people. These thoughts faded in and out, depending upon the current view, a rest stop, or personal interest.

After cranking through these miles, we finally made it to Dawson Creek, the beginning of one of our trip's highly desired - though possibly illogical - intended routes: The Alaskan Highway. We drove deliberately into town to circle the rotary that contained Milepost 0, the official beginning of the "highway". I was fairly sure its severity was more myth and legend than reality, but it was still the road to our Mecca. We rested that night in the Caravan Motel of Fort St. John, British Columbia, getting ready to run down some mileposts (and kilometerposts).

OLD AND NEW: ALASKA-CANADIAN HIGHWAY

Day 9: 406 / 3945

We were somewhat re-Americanized today. I was rather surprised, and at first I did not even make the flimsy connection to it being the Alaskan Highway. We were still in the depths of British Columbia, so there theoretically should not have been a correlation between the road's environment and the road's American-based namesake. And, granted, there probably was no correlation except for the accommodations made to American tourists in RVs. The number of flying American flags on flagpoles was somewhat surprising. The rippling power of the US could be felt best in other countries.

Within a few miles of starting out this morning, I quickly noticed how the intersections, country stores, gas pumps, and Detroit chariots (which had conquered this market) were photocopied from a generic part of any unnamed united state. Only the international symbol signs and products labeled in English with a complete repeat of everything in French told us that we were not in Kansas anymore, Toto.

The strangest thing was how the landscape had changed. The coniferous trees were taken over in great numbers by deciduous trees, giving us forests to pass through that were like our short Sunday rides at home. Even the hills themselves could have easily been mistaken for the Black Hills of South Dakota. Later in the day, the conifers regrouped and darkened the hills again.

The scenes transformed, however, and I grew very impressed with what the Alaskan Highway had to show. Even areas which were not officially labeled and zoned as "parks" could easily have passed for "park land". However, long tracts were overrun with thin-pole conifers that had some spindly greens on them so that no one would question whether they were trees or giant hairy toothpicks, all the result of poorly thinned post-logging forest growth. Many areas had the aftereffects of forest fires, including signs along the road with constant warnings. Varying degrees of re-growth or human-planned clearing and re-planting were interspersed throughout. The land slowly flowed from "America" to rolling northern forests and on to such extremes as hyperactive Badlands-bald mountains and snow-capped lunar peaks. It all required some looking, but there was a lot to find.

Valleys, mountains, and lakes along the Al-Can Highway

As to the famed Alaskan Highway rough-and-tumble hell-road myth: was it myth or was it real? For that first day the answers came from different perspectives, depending on one's mode of transport. In a pickup truck, it would have been no big deal. You just needed to plan on some nicks in the paint and possibly a star-cracked windshield. On motorcycles, the road was very rideable, but required finesse. A majority of it was roughly paved. So roughly, in fact, that I sometimes found it difficult to tell if I was coming upon gravel-covered roadway or gravelly-looking, yet firm, pavement. Loose gravel over pavement gave our bikes the jitters, and loose gravel over dirt was much worse. Simple pavement or simple packed dirt would have been just dandy for me and my mount, but presumably the frost heaves and permafrost eventually crumbled regular pavement back to gravel anyhow. At least that's what I assumed was the reason for using taxpayer money to spread out miles and tons of small rocks and dust.

I just mentioned dust. I did that for a reason: there was lots of it. Passing cars and trucks going the other way gave my lung's cilia a workout. Dad took the wild west outlaw approach and fixed a red patterned bandana around his head and over his nose and mouth. I was planning to noose myself up with one the next day too.

Dust bandana for the Bandit Biker look

We ended up in the bustling "metropolis" of Muncho Lake, which lacked people and buildings but was a good place for a rest stop. In the evening before bed I was surrounded by the insulated, log cabin style walls of a room at the J&H Wilderness Resort. Sheesh, that name was stupid. "Wilderness Resort". Nice oxymoron.

It did include a hot shower, though, along with RV hookup sites and small boat rentals for the lake. At least the shower was useful. The last hour on the road beforehand had been spent in cold rain, with Dad's BMW intermittently running on one of two cylinders. Accumulated dust and chill was solved by the hot water running down our backs, and non-firing cylinder problems were solved by a change of spark plugs that evening.

BEAUTY AND BEAST: MOTORCYCLE HELL

Day 10: 319 / 4264

The myth had become reality. We had been to Motorcycle Hell. The cast of characters: two lost souls (played by us) and The Devil (played by gravel). Location: The Alaskan Highway (the term "highway" used for humorous effect) between Muncho Lake and Morley River. Motivation: because it was there.

What a day! This actually was my favorite day yet on this trek. I did not feel so much like a traveling-through tourist, camera on a neck strap at an overlook. I really worked for the trip this day, and better yet, it was not easy.

There was sometimes still that underlying feeling of going through a somewhat tourist-ridden area when a RV towing a car would blow by, letting me enjoy its dust wake and an occasional spray of small pebbles. But, the fact that they were all blowing by us was exactly the point. Today was the first time that we literally passed no one and were passed by everyone (of course not a single one of them was on a motorcycle). We almost passed a lumber truck once, but it was only moving so slowly because it was making a turn up into a canyon. At least our record of no passes was kept unblemished; we did not even catch him before he turned into another cloud of dust heading perpendicular.

The road was occasionally paved - rough Alaska Highway style - but mostly wasn't. And you would not believe the "wasn't" parts. For a cruiser with four or more wheels, no problem. Just go slow, accumulate dirt, and look for strategic spots to pass wobbling lost souls on motorcycles. And some of them were not even going slow. And some were also not too strategic. Nobody got away clean, though.

The Universe shifted for two-wheeled landsleds. Our first encounters with 4-stroke speed skating came on gravelly sections similar to those from the day before. Just mild-out-of-controlness. Method of attack: slow down to 2nd or 3rd gear, feel bike squirm around, feel bike go in wrong direction, wiggle handlebars in some fashion that seemed appropriate, and rely on random chance to keep the rubber side down. This method worked well, even though I made a fair share of split second resignations to chewing up my jeans. It also occasionally put us in the lane of opposing traffic. The interest level always rose when traffic actually appeared and opposed. No countersteering on this stuff.

The Alaska Highway apparently decided that we were not being challenged to our abilities, so it then threw another whammy at us: same conditions, but wet. And the wet came from either our government buddies with their watering trucks or from Mother Nature with bursts of rain. Since the number of watering trucks was limited and could not follow us all day long, the trucks and rain tag-teamed throughout the day to keep us continually amused.

Wet gravel on top of wet, silty dirt. Basically, the only thing keeping me upright was a combination of Suzuki momentum and a balancing act. Rigid body, alertness, and tight grips through my leather gloves all rounded out the package. The worst part was worrying about falling and getting crushed by the tailgating, impatient RV vibrating in my rear view mirrors. I became quite adept at waving people on, around, and good riddance.

The worst came in the early afternoon. We had already survived the pothole slalom courses. And we even survived a five mile long avalanche zone beside which construction equipment was placed to make it look like we were still on a "highway". This was the only place kind enough to warn us that there was a "Rough Road" ahead sign. After having come through everything else, we did not know whether to laugh or be scared upon seeing that.

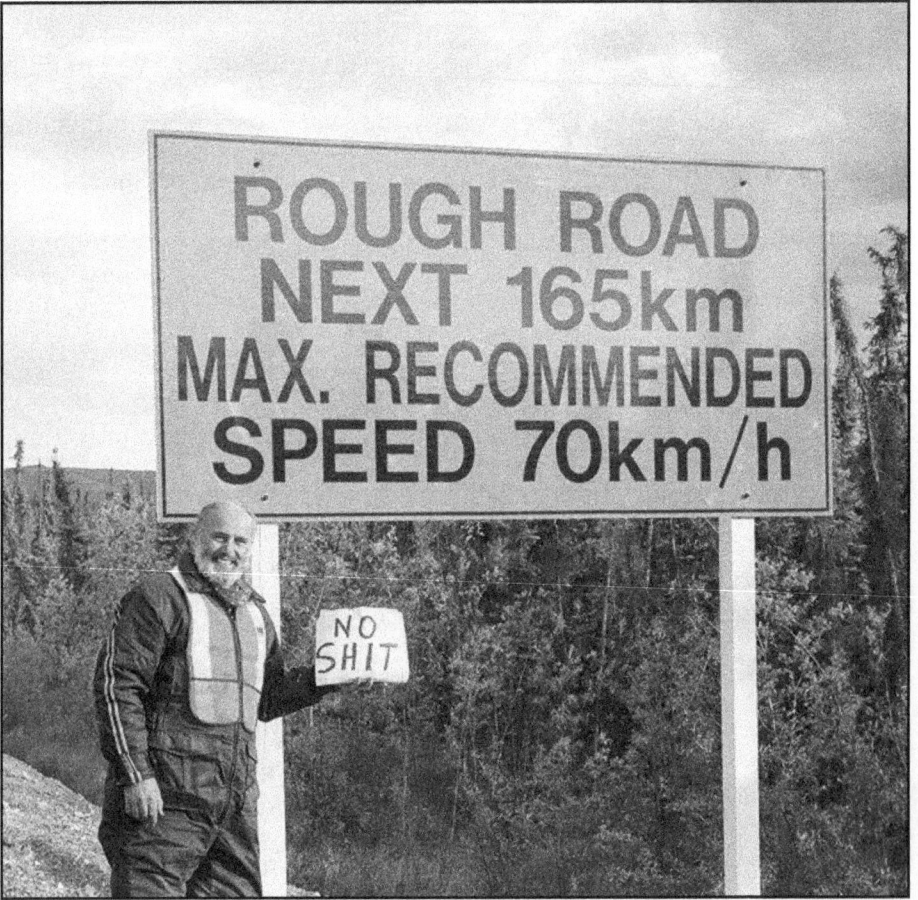

Even so, none of these obstacles were as sadistically treacherous as the Mountains of Twisty Curves Covered With Ball Bearing Gravel. All of the other problems applied there as well, but the curves added new variety. Forward momentum and wheel centrifugal force, the only physical laws that previously worked in our favor, then worked against us to try and force us off the edges of curves, into ditches, or over cliffs. That wouldn't do.

I tried using the brakes to slow myself once. The front tire locked up. "OK, don't plan on slowing down", I thought. I crested a large hill, catapulted up and down from a deep pothole, and rolled toward a sharp curve. I tried to straighten out the curve with a new trajectory, but the curve did not bend for me. I steered left with the road, the motorcycle continued its momentum right away from the road, brakes were useless, and all while accelerating faster going downhill. So I was galloping across the countryside, ending up sideways in a ditch.

My first road crash! I unfortunately had to qualify that with "road" since my parking lot drop tally was by this time at two, and hopefully holding steady. And, of course, use of the word "road" in describing this area was a matter of opinion anyhow. Nonetheless, it was a momentous event of dubious proportions.

After entering the supposedly wild territory of the Yukon, roads actually improved and transformed into something approaching a real highway. Concluding our day of motorcycle wrestling, we zonked at the Morley River Lodge. The laid back atmosphere and friendly, warm locals were a welcome treat. And a couple tall refreshing sodas felt good, too.

MOTORCYCLES AND JACKRABBITS IN PURGATORY

Day 11: 286 / 4550

Hell froze over and we made it to Purgatory, then Heaven surrounded us on all sides. The relatively gentle, manageable roads of the prior night continued on throughout the Yukon. Granted, we still had some frost heave space launches and needed to be wary of hidden-from-view-until-the-suspension-crunched potholes. There was also still some gravel, but it was always in short sections of road and the rocks were not as polished, buffed, and waxed as they were in Motorcycle Hell.

This role reversal struck my prearranged ideas as weird: the wilderness-laden name of "Yukon" had more twentieth century roadway than did the much more refined sounding name of "British

Columbia". Rumors, stories, and what tourism sold: environment as product, rather than environment as it was. Certainly the Alaskan Highway was not solely indicative of the rest of the territory, but it was indicative of how full of it predisposed ideas could be.

We fortunately again travelled away from the far reaching feel of main street America that had infiltrated into parts of the AlCan. The landscape slowly changed from the road's beginning, although many of the same variables were there the day before, only shaken up into new vials of potion. Dark rolling hills would occasionally jut out lopsided or be exposed by a cleared burn area. Interlocking mounds had charred poles covering them, looking like a magnified view of the hair on a mammal's back. And the gravel-covered road curved on and on between small towns, with occasional rough offshoot roads that always disappeared around a bend into the deep woods.

This day, however, things became even more foreign and unusually beautiful. So many things were almost like a postcard, but had a more pressing, dynamic feeling to them. The people dwindled and the Yukon showed us what "sparsely populated", "unpopulated", and "populated only by jackrabbits" meant.

Alaska-Canadian Highway through the Yukon

In a way of showing us how different this place was, over the span of several days we *twice* came upon burned out hulks of a Volkswagen Rabbit by the side of the road. The second one was enveloped in acrid smelling flames as we approached, a bonfire coming from both the interior and the engine compartment. It was surreal enough coming upon this unexplainable scene in the middle of nowhere, but stranger yet to see nobody around for miles in either direction. Not a person anywhere. We even peered inside to make sure no hapless soul's charred skeleton was there, but saw nothing except for blackened seat springs on curling vinyl. This was dangerous territory for VW Rabbits, apparently.

There had never been a problem getting fuel, but gas stops had turned into depots combining a gas station, restaurant, grocery store, and motel all together in one family run operation. We stayed in such a place that night: the Bayshore Motel and Restaurant. I overlooked pretty Kluane Lake from my desk there, but the water in my shower smelled funny. Taking the good with the not so good, to make it all great.

Dad and I pulled in needing gas. The father came out and, as had been usual in Canada, he was very friendly. We took a room with no competition from anyone else - though a few people came later – and we asked about getting a meal. Well, they had just closed up, but the wife did not mind making dinner for us. She cooked while one of her daughters served us and asked waitress questions without really being a waitress. The other daughter was outside hanging linens on a clothesline, all from the six motel rooms.

When I came back later to get a Diet Coke for Dad, the food-oriented mother and daughter were at a table by the cash register watching TV, and they were pleasantly interested in my college degree and our trip. Dad really enjoyed these non-commercialized places fueled by friendliness, and I was beginning to get a sense of why.

The Yukon also unraveled impressive scenery, bringing out mountain chains and big-sky clouds. Our travels brought the unusual feeling of having a scene's mood depend upon which way my nose was pointed. From one traveling spot I could see an incredible range of things.

Sunlit blue sky over deep green bushes and trees. Smoky gray fog over blackened hills. Blue-gray clouds overlapping brilliant white wisps and puffs, all moving over mountains patterned with crisp snow and exposed brown rock. Huge rain clouds with visible streaks of rain and cloud falling into valleys. Nebulous white-gray clouds looking like snow exploding off of the snow-capped mountains they hovered over. And all of this while riding in open sunlight with rain popping on my helmet, running across my faceshield.

Yukon Territory

Our first major mecha-medical problems occurred that day, both in the Suzuki. The BMW had given us trouble before we actually rolled and had needed some extra parts since, but the Suzuki choked up our day with roadside repair. The first problem was an easy one, though it took a while to find: nothing worked because of a fuse. We then purchased 15 extra fuses. After Dad over-bought five extras, we later found that we already had ten more while rummaging through all of our combined tools and parts collections.

After driving for about twenty five miles on a near-powerless Suzuki that barely made it up hills, Dad and I pulled into a Tastee Freez parking lot and tore apart anything tearable. Culprit: snapped-off arm of one of the two sets of points. Of course we had a spare only for the other set that still worked, but Dad cannibalized the old and the new to make a working hybrid. After a very long distance phone call to Dad's friend back home to get a mechanic's advice, my father reassembled the beast. The feel through my butt told me it was running even better than before it broke. And that was after a surgery session with minimal tools and no Suzuki dealer for who knows how many mountain chains. Good job, Dad.

HEAVES AND SMOOTH: END OF THE ALCAN

Day 12: 460 / 5010

We covered so much territory this day that everything we did seemed very far away at day's end. It did not feel as though I was in a worn and torn lodge overlooking Kluane Lake just that morning. It felt more like several days. I was not unusually tired, and we had certainly pushed back more miles in a day, but the jump from Kluane Lake to Fairbanks in Alaska seemed intuitively too large. Assuming no hallucinations, it did all actually occur though.

The AlCan – the Alaska–Canada Highway's shorthand name - diversified its interests and expanded into a new market: rolling mini dunes of frost heaves. Bouncing around in the heaviest rain of the trip so far, we experienced every one of the gut-busters that the road threw our way. I wove and meandered through rises and falls, all while trying to minimize how hard my chest's breath would be jounced and how fast the suspension would bottom out hard, metal against metal.

Many could not be avoided entirely, and sometimes avoiding one just meant slamming another. The frost heaves were not like I had expected. Yet another cut to preconceived ideas. I had thought they would be ruptures in the pavement, with fragmented pavement on top, strewn ahead by passing cars. Instead, they were quick up and down roller coaster rides, smooth but sudden. This made them sometimes difficult to spot from a distance, especially when everything grayed out under a cloud-hidden sun. I learned to read the vertical curves over time, and tell-tale signs were usually on each one: skid marks from the tires of hopping towed trailers. The black patches were very helpful as I would flow the bike into a large dip and simultaneously rise and lower myself above the seat while standing on the foot pegs.

After riding like a pogo stick this way, we finally crossed the imaginary international line into Alaska. It felt really good inside to have made it to that big objective of the trip. It had been a mysterious goal at first, going off to a big rugged state far from the reaches of home and the continental US. Then a weathered sign appeared, and it all became reality.

I immediately noticed how the sunlight seemed brighter on everything from trees to picnic tables to my soda can. And the atmosphere of the land changed quickly, too. The aspens came back in waves, the clouds were stronger, and the distant Alaska Range was younger and more challenging. Nature did not recognize international boundaries, but this was definitely something new.

Entering Alaska from the Yukon

After passing through the two minute why-even-bother US Customs inspection, the relative quality of Uncle Sam's roads became quickly apparent as well. For the first time in seemingly years, I was gliding over smooth blacktop with non-gravel shoulders and brightly painted lane lines. What a change: my steering inputs gave intended outputs, unlike a bump combined with wind gust over sliding stones to make creative random outputs.

However, all was not bliss. Motorcycle Hell oozed its way over the international line and took a foothold in an eighteen mile stretch of road. What the gravel lacked in roundness it made up for in squishy depth. And the yellow-white dust storms from passing construction trucks were invigorating, too. And I knew that M. H. would be laying low like a predator: we had to come back that way.

The people of Alaska seemed less laid back than those in Canada, but they were generally as pleasant. A little more hurried and brusque, but not by much. The shops also became specialized again, and they accepted – as Dad jokingly called it – "real money". I found myself still doing multiplication in my head, converting kilometers on signs to the miles I better understood. I had to remind myself that the conversion had already been done for me. I was creating new units.

After leaving Tok, the road straightened out for mile after mile. The only variety was up and down. Horizontally, it was 2D. Since there were no wind gusts, I simply held steady and became mesmerized. The road stayed mostly on flatlands, but I could see the Alaska Range sliding by over the trees. The Alaska Range was my favorite mountain scenery of the trip so far, with jagged outlines and snow that covered not only their peaks but filled the faces down to their bases.

We gradually approached them at an angle, and touched their foothills briefly before jutting across more flatlands to the North Pole. The North Pole was a real town, and yes they did have a bunch of hokey, touristy gimmicks that capitalized on their namesake's relationship to Santa Claus.

We then finally made it to the end of the Alaska Highway. It officially ended in Delta Junction. We had originally thought it ended in Fairbanks, and that was originally intended to be our highway finale. The contrary news was a briefly perplexing surprise, but it did not change our plans.

We stayed in Fairbanks at the Ranch Motel. Although I was writing until past 2:00 in the morning, the sky was still light. I thanked the inventor of curtains when I went to bed.

WILDLIFE AND FASHION: DENALI

Day 13: 182 / 5192

If any moose or caribou were watching me from inside that grove of bushes across the river, they must have been wondering what I was. They were probably smart enough to figure me out though, since I still fit the bipedal format.

I was sitting on the green side of a folded up space blanket. This small yet helpful "cushion" was protecting my butt from the harshness of the great rock there. The rock - craggy and shaped by the many pieces that broke off or wore away across stratified layers – had formed itself into a natural chair. The top was flattened enough for me to seat myself, and the rock sloped down from there into the river. Plenty of room to rest my feet, though I could feel the blood pumping through my heels since they were my feet's only pressure point. Maybe this setup would not have sold well in a furniture store, but Mother Nature had it patented anyway and the connecting scene could never have been packaged.

It was probably 11:30 at night, maybe later. The wind had slowed to a gentle flow, but the air became cooler as the sun fell below the mountain to my right. Looking at that mountain, I was attracted to the clouds above it. It was one of the first things I had noticed while setting up my little camp.

The colors changed more than the shapes. From the volcanic plume clouds contoured in brilliant yellow, they grew into an inferno red-orange with pastel yellows only left low in a valley. Everything else was gray-blue, including the hazy form of the mountain that I never looked at directly, using it instead as a sharp-edged frame for the clouds above.

The crescent moon was hovering in a washed-out blue sky over this river, and I noticed the sun was no longer making the snow on the mountains glow white hot. While walking down the road from our campsite and hopping around stone and mud bars in the river, I especially saw Mt. McKinley, huge and snow-covered in the distance. It was later obstructed from my view by a long, low ridge, but I knew it was still there. Just difficult to see because of distance and its self-made clouds, with white snow fading into the color of its background sky.

Dad and I had come down to this river from our site at the Savage River Campground in Denali National Park. We walked together between the gravel bars and bushes that split the river into convoluted channels. They changed course frequently over time; tearing down mud and stone, building it back up. The construction company was a constant flow of brown-green milky muddy snowmelt from mountains far away.

River meandering through a wide valley bottom in Denali

We talked about how likely it would have been for large wildlife to live here. The huge tracks of moose, as well as caribou and even bear, confirmed that. Some were relatively fresh, and many were interspersed with a collection of dark brown egg-shaped droppings. Dad predicted we would find something around the next bend, and my confirming point startled a group of eight caribou, all growing antlers with a new brown mossy texture. They darted but then stood, eventually becoming somewhat at ease with us, though frequently glancing and sometimes directly studying us with their heads held high and erect over the plants they were tearing and eating. The herd crossed the frigid river, knee-high for them, and continued foraging on the other side. Their tension dropped when we turned and walked back.

I finally put on my last layer of defense against the elements: a black leather glove on my non-writing hand. Simply another accessory to the fashionable rock-sitting cold weather gear. My body was mostly covered with black poopysuit, though my toes were getting cold in uninsulated riding boots. My naked hand was barely keeping warm through the energy of scribbling motions. The trendiest accessory, however, was the pair of shorts I had upside down on my head; I forgot to bring a hat. I could see why the uninitiated did not use shorts to protect their head. I kept getting a draft up the leg holes.

I put on my glasses for a last survey. No wildlife except for plants and an occasional bug. No matter and no problem. It had been worth coming out to the spot on the rock. And it sure made the cocoon of a sleeping bag feel good that night.

Denali was our northwest-most destination, so our sights were turned to the rest of Alaska and beyond to the Pacific Northwest…

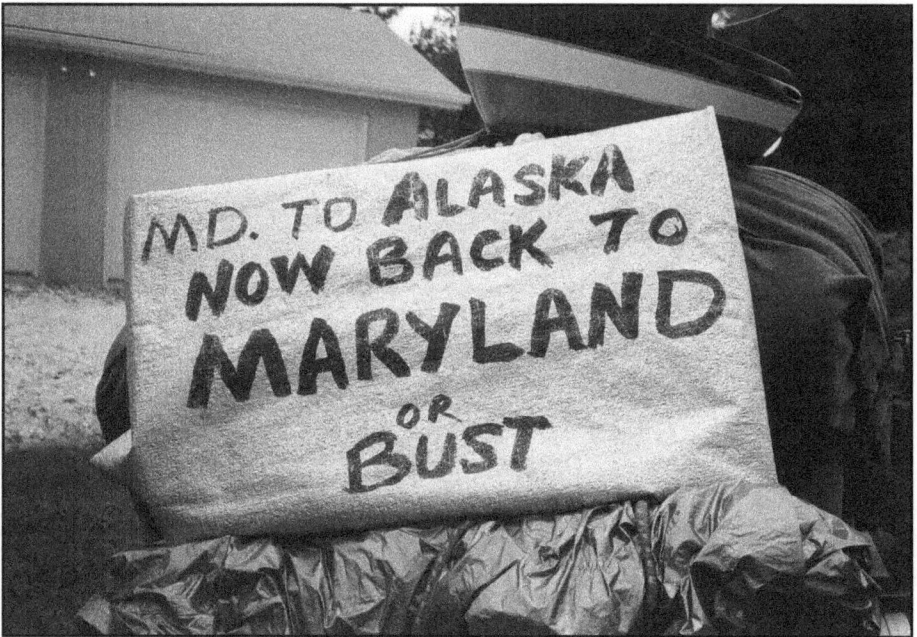

SLEEP AND CHARACTERS: DENALI TO KENAI

Day 14: 291 / 5483

I began making an intentional effort to go to sleep earlier because my tired feeling kept growing, so I made a time investment in more slumber. Occasionally I would get very drowsy on the motorcycle and even nod off. I always fought it by grunting, breathing deep, and concentrating sleepy-style, but it almost always ended with me nodding off. Survival instincts overrode hedonism and poor driving practices; a quart of adrenaline would spurt out when I realized what I was doing. Survival instincts and rolling off cliffs did not jive together. Good. I got the most painful fire hydrant supply of adrenaline this day when something in me realized that I was drifting into the lane of an opposing eighteen wheeler.

The motorcycle itself actually vibrated me to sleep. Not lulled, but vibrated. I seemed to be followed by the Vibration Monster. My body had been numbed at times by the four cylinder Suzuki buzz. That was to be expected. But even the lounge table on the ferry four days later was vibrating from the ship's huge engines and propellers. Unexpected, but I was getting generally accustomed to it all. Maybe there was a spot on a mountain in Colorado that did not vibrate. It probably had earthquakes, though.

Having not yet decided on our plan of attack, Dad and I talked around in circles about what to do and where to go. We finally decided to not decide, and instead to let it flow; we'd decide when we got to wherever. Though somewhat inconvenient, Denali had a respectable set of strict rules designed to limit traffic and therefore prevent migration of wary wildlife away from the roads.

A park bus made scheduled runs into and out of the park, all originating from the entrance at Riley Creek. Starting the very next day, runs would have gone through the whole length of the solitary park road. But that day the busses only wound half-length to Toklat. No problem with us since we would not have had time to go much further. It's a slow bus on a slow road. And we were required to clear out of our campsite, which posed a timing problem.

A ranger told us that we could park at an overlook and ride the bus from there. We waited for the bus. Then the bus came and the driver told us that we could not park there. Goodbye. We drove back to the only available parking spots, at Riley Creek. Again inconvenient, but I actually wished that more parks were as restrictive so as to preserve the relative purity of the landscape.

Denali was graced with another non-touristy feature: no hiking trails. Hiking and backpacking was allowed throughout the park via a restricted number of permits, except in wildlife sensitive areas where young were being raised or where there were known grizzly bears. But hikers made their own trail wherever a map, topography, and vegetation allowed. That's the way I liked it, though I had never actually done true long range bush whacking by that point. The beauty and wildlife ranked this as a prime returning spot for backpacking and backcountry camping. Years later, my brother and I did just that and had many more stories to tell from the experience.

We picked up tickets for the 10:30 bus, and piled on with a group of tourists stringing binoculars and Instamatics around their necks. Manmade albatrosses, I supposed. Aubrey, our driver and P.A. guide, immediately assaulted us with his personality. Brown pants, brown denim jacket, brown cowboy hat, and brown cowboy boots. All very monochromatic dark brown. He demonstrated his friendliness in a few sentences, his humor in a few jokes, and his stern insistence on following The Rules in more than a few sentences, all drawn out and solemn for effect so that they would sink into our thick heads. He finished his introduction with a loud attempt at getting us excited again to lighten the atmosphere.

Though he began as an overbearing elementary school teacher, and he had more jokes that had obviously been exhaled many times before, he turned out to be well-intentioned about his job and responsibilities. Although very serious about the whole deal, Aubrey turned out to be a good guy. He always stopped for wildlife when someone yelled the rule-phrase that he liked for its simplicity: "Stop, Aubrey!" And he wanted everyone to enjoy themselves. Smoking a cigarette with his knee bent and boot on the bus at an overlook, he told us the obligatory personal bear story. Little did I know that years later I would have my own grizzly story there, when I would be head-on charged to within just a few feet by a huge grizzly going after me and my aromatic pot of chicken noodle soup.

The paved road changed to a dirt and gravel road winding around and over the perimeter of Denali's mountains and passes. The open bushy permafrost, scattered with trees and rocky creeks, gave fine viewing for large wildlife. The lower elevation and occasional trees separated it from what elsewhere was officially called tundra, though there were shared characteristics in this ecosystem.

The wildlife did not trip into our laps, and they were still hidden well, lying low in bushes or standing in groves of trees. But the number of roving eyes onboard "The Battlestar" provided for many "Stop, Aubrey!" opportunities. "The Battlestar" was Aubrey's nickname for the amphibious looking, military angled bus.

That morning I told Dad how I had always wanted to see a grizzly bear in the wild. There were supposedly good chances of seeing them in Sable Pass, so my original suggestion of getting off the bus early to hike along the Teklanika River took a prominent place in our minds. However, the suggestion eventually passed completely out of our minds because of the variety and number of wildlife sightings we were experiencing from the road.

I wanted to see grizzlies. I saw ten: a sow and three cubs, a sow and two cubs, a sow and one cub, and a boar. One sow was protecting a moose it killed two days earlier and had buried for between-meals keeping. We saw more herds of caribou, with each separated as either male or female groups, and even saw likely the same herd we had seen the night before by the river. Dall sheep looked like small patches of snow until they moved across the slopes on dental floss thin legs; they became clearer, dotting the mountains. I hoped the fellow passengers with clicking Instamatics enjoyed dots; they would be lucky if the Dall sheep were allotted one grain of film. But then other sheep came down and even surrounded The Battlestar. Several moose and a golden eagle rounded out the collection.

Grizzly sow and cubs (lower right corner) in vast Denali

Dall sheep in Denali

Later giddying up to get going, we mounted our steeds after making the return trip from Toklat. We headed south for Anchorage. I nodded off here and there, and eventually had to stop because the constant wind dried my eyes out to the point that I couldn't open one of them again. Monocular, flat, no depth perception driving wasn't advisable.

Reinvigorated after the stop, I took notice of the effects from the low northern sun. The forested hills and cloud-islands sky were in pastel yet intensely lit blues, greens, yellows, browns, and light reds, all separated with little continuum between them.

Passing from that vista into the outskirts of Anchorage was a back-home reminder. A stinking industrial fog hovered over the road as our welcome arch, and the buildings and businesses quickly multiplied. No family outposts there, only McDonalds. The Alaskan form of hurry was in the air and evident in the running streams of vehicles.

Searching the entire town for a room, and finding "No Vacancy" everywhere for some mysterious reason, we kept heading south late into the evening. Our goal for the next day had been the Kenai Peninsula; we got there a day early.

The late night trip was worth the effort: rounded mountains rose directly out of the water's edge. Dense, dark clouds loomed as one huge mass above. Foggy gray covered the peaks, hiding whatever was back in the spaces between mountains. Ending the evening as the only tenants at the Scottish Inn of Bird Creek, we had a road trip dinner of chips, candy bar, and soda, topped off with sleep for dessert.

GUNKHOLING: KENAI TO GLENN HIGHWAY

Day 15: 331 / 5814

I woke to a different alarm this morning: a piss and flush with the bathroom door wide open. When he wanted me to get up, Dad usually pushed out a drawn out series of bodily sound effects until I squirmed around in my covers. Unfortunately, the early alarm was indicative of the rest of the day; I was tired in two ways.

I was tired in the usual, sleepy sense since we had been operating mostly on Dad's sleep schedule and not on mine. He slept fewer hours than me, plus on top of that I wrote for a long time after he went to sleep. The early-to-rise approach jarred with my circadian rhythms and showed its ugly side this day. It made me drowsy and somewhat apathetic.

My other tired: I was tired of so many miles. Obviously, reality and time constraints made that imperative; I fully realized that. But I constantly wanted to hike and take meditative time at each spot… spots that we sometimes had to just roll through. If anything, though, I had a great list of places to explore in the future at a more relaxed pace. The magnitude and length of our trip became very apparent, only to be aggravated by sleepiness.

Dad and I went further into the overcast-gray Kenai Peninsula. The weather was constant drizzle, which intensified to hard rain on the entire length of our turnaround trip back out towards Anchorage. We, for some unfathomable reason, kept our rainsuits dry and warm inside our bags.

The poopysuits served as our weather armor, and the "armor" became soaked completely through. My gloves were squishy and I had to click my faceshield partially open to air out the condensing fog of breath. My face was splattered with rain and the whirling misty turbulence left in the wake of cars ahead.

The waterways and mountains of Kenai seemed to have their own weather, as it stopped raining as soon as we were away from them. We kept our wet clothes on to air them dry, making for a cool evaporative ride. One thing I did remove at a wet rest stop: my rubber booties. They had been on the outside of my pant legs, so the rain and road grunge ran down into them and filled with brown water. I took one off – tipped it over and *splash* on the ground. Same for the other. They had done more collecting than protecting.

Shore of the Kenai Peninsula

We followed the road to its terminus at the ocean in Seward. A recreational site attracted Dad's interest, so we slowly slid along a potholed, wet-slick dirt road. Nothing much there though, except for a fish hatchery and another nice view, so we headed back to town and ate ice cream cones under a storefront's overhanging protection. Sitting on the sill below the store's display windows, passers-by must have thought we were construction workers on break with our rainsuit-looking non-rainsuits and our fluorescent orange safety vests.

Heading back out, we took an offshoot onto Exit Glacier Road. The road was a similar concept to the one going to the recreational site, just a few sharp turns added here and there for slick-braking fun. Exit Glacier was very interesting, as it was more visibly a river of ice than the slushy snow leading edge of the Athabasca Glacier had been. The huge, melting convoluted pillars and boulders of ice flowed down a valley between two mountains, ending in a milky, green-white stream filled with rocks and fine glacial flour. The glacier in all its forms. The ice, because of its hard-packed crystal structure, looked as though it had been air-sprayed with the brilliant blue food coloring of a snowcone.

The large number of people who walked up to us just to talk or ask questions continued to amaze us, and it was an ongoing treat of the trip. The combination of dirty motorcycles, laden-down packs, Maryland license plates, funny looking safety suits, and clean-cut father-son appearance must have all been particularly inviting. Dad theorized that many people were inwardly yearning for a similar trip on our form of locomotion; this was probably a large part of the truth. The unusualness of our situation added flavor also. I felt it was too bad that the good looking group of college women did not share that draw. There was a "scoping for chicks" scarcity in Canada, though it only proved distracting in the US.

It was rain from there on out to Anchorage, pouring out of clouds that passed through mountains and barely clipped the peaks. The bushy vegetation covering the mountains looked like moss on a rock, at least until it all came up to the road's near edge and showed its actual large size. The mud ripples and eaten-away streambeds in the receded bays' bottoms kept holding my eye. And everything was wet.

Our mini caravan passed through Anchorage again and we had a meal at Godfather's Pizza, which was really just an excuse to change our wet socks. The day was topped off with a mad rush to a Texaco station for the worst case of diarrhea in my life. My left eyelid even puffed up and oozed for some unknown reason, perhaps because I was so full of shit. I told Dad that I would rather travel more miles tonight than get up early the next morning, so we took that approach.

We found the Glenn Highway, which I had read good things about. It did not disappoint that night or the next day. An eerie half-light showed us the way through wet shiny-slick twists in the lush mountains. Thin layers of clouds obscured strips of mountain, moving around and through, with others covering down from the top.

Palmer presented us with the King Mountain Lodge. For twenty dollars we got a doghouse stuffed with a musty sofa and a bed which was labeled as a double only because it had two pillows. We walked outside to the community bathroom located in a separate building, away from the outhouse. I slept on the floor in a sleeping bag, and the floor felt lumpy. So I lifted up a corner of the carpet to investigate; the carpet was laid directly on top of the earth with no floor in between.

Nighty night, sleep tight, don't let the bed bugs bite…

AWAKENED TO THE PEOPLE OF GLENN HIGHWAY

Day 16: 453 / 6267

Someone declared Sunday to be a day of rest, and I sent thanks. I felt much better, actually waking Dad up for the first time on the trip. When the light streamed in through the thin doghouse curtains, I felt good.

We drove more non-stop miles, but I enjoyed it much more than the prior few days. An alert mind always helped. The Glenn Highway played a great scenery movie, and the road was motorcycle curvy. The southwest section was a nicely paved winding road through mountains, after which the northeast section became bumpier and the mountains and glaciers became distant. The happy dilemma of the day: enjoy the scenery or enjoy the road.

Getting hungry, we pulled off to a roadside café. The backside of a building presented itself, but an arrowed sign said "We're open – come around!" We did, and later found that the road had been moved from the front of the building to a new, straighter route behind. The old highway now served as the café owner's driveway.

A large, built-up shack housed the café, kitchen, bathrooms, and bar. We had our pick of the three tables since we were the only customers, except for a younger family member taking up one third of the table selection while reading a newspaper. A friend of the owner's wife, who was on an extended visit from Tennessee, served us in a genuine and friendly way. I could hear her prepare everything we had ordered since the kitchen was right beside us, around the edge of an open doorway.

When she came out with food or a soda can, I needed to consciously avert my eyes from her pronounced half-circle belly. Talking to her was pleasant, though she sometimes randomly switched to aloof. The owner, wearing a cap and beard and sipping a cup of coffee at the bar, told us about the problems of small business in these little traveled parts of Alaska. Not just lack of customers – that was expected and accounted for – but also the rules made in Juneau that favored the big numbers operations. Dad agreed from his experiences as a small business owner, and we left with a pleasant "Stop in again sometime" following us out the door.

The Glenn Highway emptied out onto the AlCan, where we backtracked to Haines for the intercoastal ferry. Our speeds were faster than coming; we had seen this stretch before and were cranking out miles again. The change in direction definitely changed the view, however. The sun was not in our eyes. The mountains on our traveling side of the road took new prominence over those on the left. A section of forest looked dark and ominous, hiding something back in the branches. Most of our attention was on the frost heaves, which were coming upon us much quicker this time. The swerves were more severe and the suspensions were repeatedly mushed and bottomed out. Of course, the gravel and potholes had not left, either.

Due to the lateness of the hour - and not wanting to get stranded without a dinner - we stopped into another café. A mildly wispy-in-the-head man took our orders. I thought he was interesting, but Dad could not handle the "space cadet".

The woman who owned the café cooked up our vittles from an open, visible kitchen. She showed who was in control when two Americans tried to con the third person there, an older man who worked the gas pumps, talked, and watched TV between business. We never figured out what all the heated arguments were about, though it was obvious it had something to do with change that was given and the exchange rate. We saw the plump argument-initiating couple later at the Kluane Wilderness Village; they moved on because it was deemed too expensive. The Prices stayed.

FINE COMPANY: TO HAINES AND THE ALASKA MARINE HIGHWAY

Day 17: 271 / 6538

D ad knew exactly where he wanted to go: back to the Bayshore. That was the family-run operation where we previously stayed, overlooking Kluane Lake. He really enjoyed the atmosphere and people in these places, and a good breakfast was on the agenda.

The mother (cooking) and daughter (fixing, waitressing, and serving) remembered us well, and talked to us between their busy runs. All six tables were filled, including a group of elderly women on a stuffed-van tour led by an outgoing man in his fifties. The man and his group were full of zip and helped pass the waiting time quickly. One woman had even lived fifty years ago in Dawson City, a small town in the northern Yukon (different from Dawson Creek). Her return visit on this trip was nostalgic and especially interesting in one respect: she said the town had hardly changed.

The meal was good and filling. The mother and daughter stood at the doorway until we left, impressed by how far this journey had already taken us. They perhaps had wistful thoughts of themselves traveling far away for a while, thinking how and if they would actually do it.

The AlCan zoomed us along again, all the way back to Haines Junction and to the same Tastee Freez parking lot that served as our Suzuki-fixing "garage" previously. The Tastee Freez man, remembering us, could not believe that it had been a week. Looking back at the time, I agreed: it was hard believing it had been an eight day gap. But the proof was there. Haines Junction served well as a junction, and we took a new direction down the Haines Highway.

The road was well paved except for a length of heavy, rough construction. Midway through, a construction worker stopped us seemingly just for the purpose of genuine pity. He said "It's only five more miles". Only five. You could have been a pessimist or an optimist on that one. Past the construction, the rain caught up with us again and we – again – did not wear our rainsuits. We again got wet. It was very nice having useful equipment serve as useless weight. Our rationale had usually been either a) it might pass soon, or b) we were already wet and could not get much wetter without drowning, so just keep going.

Haines, a drizzly little town, had the shops we needed. A laundromat served as our weather haven. Dad watched the laundry spin and re-packed some bags while I went to a grocery store and bagged up snacks for the upcoming ferry voyage. We then took our cleaned clothes and did some pseudo-strategic packing. We organized things to be used while onboard and transferred them into our tank bags and camp equipment bags. Things not to be used were stuffed in our saddle bags, to be left on our bikes in vehicle stowage below deck for the three day ferry voyage.

Pizza topped with sprouts (a poor attempt at making the slimy meal nourishing) served as dinner, and the crew of two was ready to board. While eating pizza, a nice tall man wearing black bad-ass motorcycle clothes, red-brown hair, and a big red nose walked into the pizza joint and introduced himself. He was riding a Gold Wing motorcycle through Alaska, and had been walking around town waiting for the ferry. Like us, he was going the entire distance to the Seattle area, though from there he was on his way to home and wife near San Francisco.

We ended up hanging out, talking, and eating meals with this man, Nat, for days afterwards. Fortunately, he was not just all-motorcycles, talking and talking on and on about two wheeled beasts. He had many interesting things to say about logging, construction, his work as a Teamsters truck driver, travels, and people. Self-described as a loner, but he was a friendly loner.

The wait for boarding vehicles passed quickly, talking to people from the head of the line in our position reserved for motorcycles. There was one more bike, ridden by a military guy just out of college and touring through to his new assigned location in Arizona. Everyone else in line was packed into a car, pickup/4X4, or RV. After about forty five minutes, we straddled and rode across the gratings onto the steel floor of the ferry's vehicle stowage area.

I immediately grabbed the camping gear bags and headed topside while Dad stayed behind and secured the bikes with ropes so they wouldn't fall over in rough seas. I had been told by several people that the Solarium was the prime spot for passengers without staterooms. Dad and I had decided to forego a room and instead use the money for more hotels along the road elsewhere. I would not have minded more camping on the road, but the convenience, beds, time savings, and showers were always appreciated at motels. Having had the Solarium pointed out to me from the parking lot, I followed stairs that ascended in the general direction up to the top deck and all the way aft. I quickly found it.

The reason for its popularity was in the overhead heaters. Although the rear side of this large open area filled with lounge chairs was exposed to the sea wind, the space heaters took some of the bite out of it. I had expected difficulty in finding a spot, but found a good spot by a window midway in. It was not too close to the wind and not too close to the loud industrial fan sucking air down to the engine room.

The Solarium was three quarters filled with people from the first stop on this route, Skagway; they were trying and sometimes succeeding to sleep. Except for a couple tents, all were bundled against the wind in sleeping bags on lounge chairs, with packs strewn around. Light came in from the ferry terminal and the orange glow of space heaters. I unfurled our mats and sleeping bags, then waited for Dad. Nat arrived with him and pulled up a lounge chair. After getting situated and watching the ferry push away, we zonked at around one o'clock in the morning with blankets around our heads as protection from the cool breeze, rocked to sleep as the ferry headed south.

Sleeping arrangements on the Alaska ferry: funky bed, great view

AFLOAT: ALASKA PANHANDLE BY FERRY

Day 18: ~500 by ferry / 7038

After a cool night of off and mostly on sleep, I was awakened by a violin. My groggy yet inquisitive mind first asked what that screeching moan was. After the fog cleared in my head, I realized its origin and looked around for the rude jerk. Some lady who - in the course of a half hour – barreled straight through her entire repertoire. The benefits of civilization for her became obvious: she was not forced to walk the plank, or even asked to stop and go play elsewhere by the dozens of people still trying to sleep. The sound was not even good or enjoyable to hear, and she probably thought she impressed us with her early morning virtuosity. Nope; definitely nope.

A little boy, who probably owned the noisemaker, played afterwards with stronger musical timing and far more interesting music. But it was still early, and I'd rather have had it on CD at home when I was not asleep. Large groups were made of individuals, and each had an individual viewpoint. Fine, just take the viewpoint below deck when it was loud and still early.

Forced awake by sound and not choice, I walked down two decks to the public showers. I found two surprises: plenty of hot water and no line. Hallelujah to both. After that point, my whole day was the laziest on record.

I had been looking forward to a full day of rest from the vibrating steed; that Second Coming came. I relaxed on lounge chairs and stared off at passing coastline so much that it was almost ridiculous. Back in Boston or at home I would have kicked myself in the butt for not doing something more "constructive", but instead I whittled away time minute by minute entranced by the passing natural coastline. On the ferry I had no books to read, no movies to watch, no work to do, and no appointments to keep. No anything, no nothing. I could have offered to swab the decks or batten down the hatches, but I was not that nautically inclined. A day for writing, relaxing, being in place. Plan, but not much delivery. Thank goodness for today's days.

I did talk to Nat and other Solarium campers. And, while most people took a bus into Sitka, Dad and I zonked for a couple hours in the afternoon making up for lost time to violin recitals. The zonking was a quality zonk, and I woke up refreshed though just as lazy.

Food was provided during the day at a limited snack bar. It's real culinary specialty was play-for-a-quarter video games, though. There was enough to get the basics and it provided milk, yogurt, and other good USRDA foods. Snacks came from our pre-boarding grocery store cache. A big stuffer meal came in the dining room for dinner: an all-you-can-eat buffet. We gluttoned to satisfaction and moved on, this time with an excuse for laziness (digesting a big meal).

That night was colder than the prior one on the open ferry deck. I bundled up in a sleeping bag covered with a blanket. That made my body too hot, but my head was providing passages for me to breathe through out in the wind. After hunkering down as far as possible without re-breathing already exhaled air, I decided on more head protection instead. Hmmmm... How could this heat-sucking wind situation have been improved? Aaaahhhhh... The lounge chairs that nobody were using... I tilted one over on its side and tied the sleeves of a windbreaker jacket to it, resulting in a freestanding windbreak. Not balmy, but certainly a better night's sleep.

RELAXED PACE: OPENING HORIZONS

Day 19: ~500 by ferry / 7538

The days, times, and places on the ferry ride were already blurring together. I was trying to remember what happened this day as opposed to the day before, or simply just what happened. The captain and crew were taking care of the important jobs. I was responsible for personal hygiene and not falling overboard. The ferry floated us closer to Seattle.

The sun woke me this morning. The violin noisemaker apparently jumped ship yesterday, much to the relief of my ears and circadian rhythms. Or maybe she was tossed overboard in the middle of the night. The hours of sleep were not quite up to where I wanted them, but a solid late morning nap cured that. Dad said he came by several times and I never stirred when he rustled or someone else barked. The sun went behind clouds, and I was bundled comfortably. The noise from the group was mellow, and the rest was history. My neck became somewhat stiff later in the day, probably from a combination of cold and a slight upward incline to the head-end of my lounge chair bed. But that was the only adverse aftereffect. Even the personal temporary need for laziness as a way of life receded, though it stayed on as reality.

The Alaskan panhandle coastline continued to slide by during the day, and at night we were rumbling by Canada. Bald eagles flew in and out of thick trees. Bound-together timber floated in river catch areas or was collected into a corral and push-pulled down a waterway by tug boats. Nat explained how the system of floating timber worked, as well as different logging practices.

Nat was a very interesting fellow, and he had a lot of good things to say about the things he knew best. It came with a jovial, loud sense of humor that grew to be endearing. Rough around the edges, but polite and well meaning, even shyly Puritan sometimes. When Nat scanned with his binoculars, it always presented the opportunity for a conversation about something new. He made an easy friend, and he always had a story to tell.

Days began to center more around meals. I had another USRDA lunch before a tasty dinner of lingcod, rice, rolls, salad, and peas. My appetite had not been of much volume on the ferry but I had not broken a sweat burning up calories either.

I did feel very slightly sick in my stomach, possibly seasick. It happened when I was writing in the confines of the lounge, and faded when in the dining room with its large, open view windows. The slight rock of the boat may have been Public Enemy #1, but I had never been seasick before on other boats. The enclosed quarters and lack of a visual sense of the outside horizon likely made the difference. Or I may have eaten something that did not jive with my system. A mystery of insignificance.

The people onboard continued to open horizons for me. I talked for a while to a blonde-haired, round-spectacled man with an outdoorsy backpacker look. Funny stories about drinking with loggers and being hit on by old, drunk Indian women. Nat and Dad joined in, and the stories got somewhat loud for my tastes, considering the people who were trying to sleep. But it was fun, at least until I got indirectly pushed out of the conversation when it turned to drinking and hookers. Interesting subjects, but Nat and the new guy had real stories that I could only laugh and nod at.

NEW VIEWS FROM MY SHIPMATES

Day 20: ~300 by ferry / 7838

A nother day rolling on the ferry, slowly up and down and side to side. Another day hanging out. Yup. Time for a nap. Time to get to the bathroom. Time to straighten up my sleeping bag. Uh oh. That took exertion. Time for another nap.

The sleeping became better each night, probably from a combination of growing accustomed to the ferry's ambiance plus being surrounded by a quieter crowd. My head still woke up cold and not quite right, as if the blood flow in my body had changed to heat my head more and my head muscles were tensed all night. That was an inefficient way to add heat with entropy. As usual though, the somewhat unbroken chunk of sleep at night was not enough, especially with no hungry tigers around to keep me vertical and running. So the ferry solution was to be horizontal and take one extended nap during the day, with extra shut-eye time to accumulate enough sleep hours overall. Scheduling the nap was at my leisure of course, since everything on the ferry was done at my leisure. If I needed to relieve myself in the men's room, my options were open on timing, route, and duration of relievement.

The most interesting part of this ferry trip continued to be the other passengers. Nat told me more stories about trucking and life in California. While Andy, the blonde backpacker, simply bullshitted about bullshit.

A nurse from Anchorage occupied a lot of my time. She told stories of her special group that did long distance medical rescues for people on fishing boats, trapped on mountainsides, or other oddball places as needed. She would hop on a jet and travel a thousand miles for four or five hours to a small gravel airstrip on one of the Aleutian Islands. A person who had fallen into a crab cooker or cut off a hand would be waiting for them, assuming that the Coast Guard had already done its part. Gruesome stuff usually, especially considering that they only travel on these multi-thousand dollar flights for bad cases, and the people waiting had been bleeding to death or oozing from burns for many hours already.

She worked seven days on and seven days off, with two five-week vacation periods per year. Not a bad schedule at all. She enjoyed the large amount of off time because she generally disliked people yet loved traveling with her husband and two young sons.

Being a nurse and mother while disliking people was a contradiction, but she wanted to retire in a few years (though only in her forties) and buy a home in the mountains far away from everyone. She certainly loved her kids, though. She was thinking of even switching her job to be a school nurse so she could work when her kids were in school, and then travel with the family in the summer. Her husband, a CPA, could have worked overtime in the tax season and gallivanted off with her afterwards in the summer too. It was all getting planned out, and she seemed the type to actually do it if she felt the strengthening urge.

Another guy, in his early twenties and from Seattle, was a good American boy representation of Alfred E. Neuman's face. He was returning from his job in the Aleutian Islands working for a joint Soviet-American fishing company. I got him talking with the nurse. They even shared a watered down dislike for people. He wanted to like people, but tired of them easily.

A job with outdoor equipment store REI was all lined up for the upcoming summer, taking him as a guide to trek through southern areas of the Soviet Union. Quite the summer job. Having majored in Russian and being interested in the Soviets, he wanted to organize something around that. He predicted the markets would grow between the US and USSR. He was looking for opportunities to pursue, but realized the generality of his idea and current lack of opportunities, so a mildly directed aimlessness was his new way of living.

The person I enjoyed talking with most – and was most attracted to - was blonde and from Sweden. Of course, right? Not necessarily. She was pretty in the way I liked pretty: a real, no makeup appearance that looked as good when she woke up as she did the night before. OK, that was the initial attraction, but a late night talk with her on the bow woke me up to a very in-tune person. At the least, she was in tune to my wavelengths, which may or may not be considered out of tune.

Osa was the first person in my life who noticed clouds like I did. We were watching from the bow behind the Solarium, with cold wind beating at our backs to just below the point of shiver. The moon was harsh and most everyone else was asleep, but we were fine with being popsicles and had one of the most relaxed, enjoyable conversations ever. I was half seriously thinking that perhaps I should move to Sweden.

NEW ENVIRONMENT: TO THE OLYMPIC PENINSULA

Day 21: 178 / 8016

A fter being up late with Osa the night before, the early morning arrival in Seattle was way too early-morning. Since we were jumping ship, I didn't even have the chance to make a nap appointment. I knew I'd be dodging an eighteen wheeler or two. That did not literally happen, but a short night of sleep with a cold head kept me rather uninvigorated for the rest of the day.

After stuffing and packing, I chatted with fellow Solarium campers while we watched Seattle come close and its panorama slowly washed by us. Skyscrapers, zipping cars, city pace, the whole deal. The guy with Russian interests was coming home, but he predicted it would lose its shine in about two weeks. Then he would want out, back to the wilder parts. Andy was glad to be taking a train instead of a plane back to Wisconsin. The train would take him longer to get back to his job. The nurse's family did not care. They still had many weeks in their vacation and had not even fully decided where to go. Osa was somewhat apprehensive about going to New York, Washington DC, and Florida, especially after hearing many stories about the west being more beautiful than the east, with the east's hubbub and lack of laid back attitude. But she was ready to see friends and family there. Plus, one apparently just had to go to New York City.

The motley band of deck campers - brought together in a confined space yet open to the world for three days - all shook hands and said our goodbye-forevers. The motorcyclists went down to the "car deck" (named that way out of a terrible social prejudice). Using a sharp knife, we cut and hacked away the spider web of ropes that had held our bikes together steadily. Nat gave a warm, friendly goodbye, kindly adding that we were the best part of his trip. He was heading for home – arrival in two days – but an extra day here or there wouldn't have bothered him at all.

The Suzuki's battery was practically dead. The kick starter got us out and onto a commuter ferry heading across Puget Sound to Bremerton. It dropped us off after having a disgustingly sweet cinnamon bun and a short nap on the way.

We had finally made it to the Olympic Peninsula, one of the best visits on our journey. Gas and lunch powered us around the perimeter of Olympic National Forest and Olympic National Park. I loved the beauty and grandeur of the mountains, water, and forests. Even the houses provided unique visual possibilities. I first thought that this was a place to return with a camera in the future; yet it actually did far more and planted a seed that grew. I moved to Seattle nine years later.

Our first main stop came at Hurricane Ridge, based on a strong suggestion by Mom from her own previous trip there. Great suggestion. The drive up into the mountains became progressively colder as we rose. The road etched itself into steep mountainsides filled dark with towering conifers packed tight. Winding through contours and blasted-out tunnels, the air was fresh and damp.

Visibility was supposedly excellent from the ridge in general. From there, visibility spanned more than 31 miles over 95 percent of the time. Our time: we could barely see across the parking lot. I enjoyed that though, since it added eerie atmosphere to the place and removed it from being just an overlook. Occasional breaks in the clouds slowly revealed mountains several miles away, sometimes lit from sun above. Glaciers packed their valleys and clouds bunched up against their faces. A hike around Hurricane Ridge showed us many too-tame deer and quick-twitching chipmunks, as well as varieties of dwarf meadow flowers in yellow, blue, purple, red, pink, white, and other bright colors. The ridge occasionally looked like the edge of a foggy abyss, while at other times cleared to show fields covered in bright white snow and contrasting dark green trees.

Our way back to Port Angeles was wet, but the wet-producing clouds gave the ride a mysterious quality. The road acted as a surreal anti-tunnel of steam rising solidly off the pavement into the air above for twenty feet.

Being tired and ready to eat a light meal, we parked for the night at the Uptown Motel. An episode of "Beauty and the Beast" and an interesting roundtable discussion by TV's new fad-breed of sensationalist glop journalists kept our attention while we heated canned foods in a teapot on a camp stove inside our room.

SPECIAL PLACES: THE COAST

Day 22: 203 / 8219

Although Mecca at the end of our road had been Alaska, I had begun looking forward to seeing the Washington and Oregon coasts as well. The trip's farthest point had gone the way of the intercoastal ferry, but the aesthetic highlights were rocking and waving around Washington. The coast with its frothy waves pounding on sand and smooth-worn stones, and its rock block pillars shooting out from the up and down water, was a favorite.

There were many mountains and valleys in the world, but few places like the Washington coast. I enjoyed a place I could watch and experience, instead of simply view. The sound, roll, and flop of waves - from way out and moving into the beach – gave it dynamism. The power could be seen in the blowing sea mists and the huge tree trunks pushed back from the beach to the resisting steepness of the land. The mists were cool and constant, while not fishy or sticky. The driftwood trees were battered, chunked, de-barked, and de-limbed, forming a landlocked logjam above the high tide line. Jumping from one to another, some would roll, some were partially buried, and most were too large to even notice my presence. Air-sack bulbs of green and yellow bull kelp laid on the beach, with shapes ranging from pliable hay to leather whips. Outcast rock towers were dark and wet at their lower edges, with higher patches of grass and a tree on ledges at their mounded tops.

The Pacific edge was serene in its power, controllable at a distance by mere avoidance. I could have spent many hours there thinking, or watching, or writing. A house above would have helped my frame of mind, and an extended trip of hiking and camping nearby could always have been an outlet.

Dad and I had originally planned on going to Mt Rainier and Glacier National Park. I did not want to heap on any more mountain vistas or "just passing through" stops, so we changed those plans. He asked what I wanted to do with our remaining time here, so I told him: travel further along the coast into Oregon.

Waves, waterfall, and sea stacks of the Washington coast

Miles of unpopulated primordial beaches

After having a stand-up meal of packaged goods in a small grocery store, we headed back out into the drenching rain. We had driven practically nonstop to La Push, on the Quileute Indian Reservation, for our deluxe industrial meal. The rain began quickly, and reinforced my preconceptions of this being a rainy area. After about a quarter of our day's share of rain, I finally pulled out the dead weight rainsuit and actually put it around my body. I was already damp, but found that the darn thing actually performed a function. Dad did not use his, so he became soaked to the skin. It was strange how we seemed allergic to them, even though they worked so well.

We backtracked and pulled into the Third Beach parking area, with a clearing sky and drying clothes. The hike turned out to be only wet from leaf drips and a mushy rain forest floor, but not from any direct rain drops. I had expected a clammy, wet-here-and-there hike, but it was instead dry and comfortable.

A trail led us through the lush undergrowth and towering trunks of a thriving forest sprawling over rich, damp soil. It emerged onto washed-up trees and further to the rumbling beach. An amazing sight.

Perched atop a rock sea stack on the Washington coast

After having walked down the beach and climbed a steep-sided rock for a photo modeling session, Dad noticed a moving lump. We walked up to a baby seal, staring at us through sand-covered black eyes and voicing out a sound literally like "Ma, Ma". I had seen a sign saying that sometimes seal pups are left behind while their mothers feed on fish, and the mothers return later. Good, because this cute little critter deserved to be taken care of. I kneeled down about six feet away, and it wiggled across the sand directly at me. It sniffed at me some, stared up, and continued repeating "Ma". It did not know how to respond to me, but prodded toward me with its snout, possibly for food. Sorry, the camera I was clicking in its face was not very nourishing.

We left the seal and continued on a hike up ladder-like steps and into a "tropical" path lined by vertical rock, decomposing trees, and moist life in all directions. After turning around at an arbitrary point and returning to a log that the baby seal was shade-sleeping under, we wondered why the mother had not returned yet.

Seal pup on Washington coast

We stopped at the first grocery store we later found, all in an effort to relieve our parched bodies. I flipped over a seal postcard and for some bizarre reason literally the only thing the postcard said was that "many seals are abandoned by their mothers". That was not what the sign said or what I learned more about later, but at that point my level of concern rose sharply. So I told Dad to pull into the next ranger station so we could report the "abandoned" baby seal. They would presumably know what to do or, most likely, what not to do. Dad instead immediately called the station nearest the beach. The nice ranger told him of several other reports, but also that mothers can be gone for a long time. The pups should almost always just be left alone. She was sincerely thankful for our concern, and the matter was at least now off our minds and on the mind of the Park Service. Hopefully its mother came back.

I rode in the lead position down 101 south. We stopped briefly at something the sign said was "Big Cedar Tree". I wanted to see what a Big Cedar Tree was like. I found out. It was a big cedar tree. Interesting, but not impressive enough after having been through massive forests elsewhere. Impressive by itself though.

We rolled on through well paved, twisting road. The sides were lined high by sloping-away trees and huge stalked conifers with branches that didn't even start until a hundred feet up the trunk. These forests were eerie. Looking into them revealed one of the darkest daytime blacks I had ever seen. The dense and packed forest blocked out light to the ground, making a haven for nothing by imaginary monsters slithering around tree trunks. I found myself trying to make my eyes adapt, but they would not. It was a black black.

Our second jump onto the coastline was at Ruby Beach. Another beautiful area, different with its larger rocks and seaward-flowing stream. The college girls there provided an actually unwanted but unavoidable distraction. This area was easily accessible when compared to Third Beach, and that was obvious by the presence of at least twenty people. An extension of the overlook mentality: ease of doing.

Climbing over rocks and then onto our bikes, we headed south for an enjoyable evening ride to Aberdeen. The Flamingo Motel waited for us with a room. A too-big meal in town stuffed my stomach. Tomorrow: more coast!

FATIGUE AND LOOPING THE CIRCLE: HEADING EAST

Day 23: 232 / 8451

A mild case of scenery burnout got into my veins this day. A few spots on the coast, marshlands, and twisting roads were at least as amazing as usual, likely even better. However, we had been doing this for quite a while now and had seen so much. Possibly too much to properly assimilate, and my brain was giving off a physical signal for a respite. Things that happened a few days ago seemed distant, and things from weeks ago seemed abnormally near. There had been so much to think about on this trip that the mental pileup was growing jumbled.

I had told Dad about my interest in slowing the pace a bit and absorbing more, and he proposed an understanding, concerned way of doing that within the constraints of our planned time. Mt Rainier and Glacier were deleted from our itinerary to allow more time on the Oregon coast for sitting on driftwood and skipping smoothed rocks across waves. I thanked him for that, and hoped he was enjoying the non-tour-bus method as well.

I believed my disease had come from a need to relax and do some normal, relatively boring things. I only needed that for a little while, but it let my mind regain momentum and sort out. A lesson: there were virtues to reading a newspaper and seeing a movie on the VCR. I had never thought to the contrary, and I did not consider either to be brainless pastimes, but the therapeutic effects of occasional normalcy and repetition had become apparent. I could certainly only handle doses of that relaxation and ritual for a finite amount of time, but the benefits of balance were needed.

If I were alone and had unlimited time for the trip, then a few days of new theater movies, getting updated on world news, and reading a novel would have been nice. Refreshed, I could then continue on brightly. Although this continued to be an amazing trip, I was feeling ready to begin reorienting the trek's direction homeward. The future would return me to many of these locations and the many we may have missed or passed around. The experiences were already broadening my sight considerably.

A cool, dotted-cloud day greeted us and our poopysuits. Occasional drizzle, but nothing to soak in. The path from Aberdeen took us for a looped excursion away from 101 onto 105, which ended back around on 101.

Westport was a busy little fishing town that had tourist overtones. Fishing charters, fishing poles, fishing tackle, and supposedly fish all filled the area. I had noticed a human obsession with fishing ever since first crossing into Canada actually. The attraction alluded me, but it apparently grabbed many others. The town's Pacific beach pounded away, gray overcast. It lacked the form and beauty of Third Beach, but was engrossing in its broad open stretches and linear simplicity.

Riding south, the scenery became less momentous, though the gargantuan Christmas tree farms and the wet-saturated farmland was visually intriguing. Marshy inlets, with their covering grasses and wading herons, were unique wildlife ecosystems. But I had expected the road to twist directly beside the coast, instead of being a good ways inland. Between the visual bangs, I felt as though I was wandering with no specific goal for a destination, looking for something as it came upon me. That would not normally have bothered me at all, but my condition fed upon it.

I was reinvigorated by spending time on the beach of beautiful Ecola State Park. A roller coaster ride road heaved and sunk us down away from the highway to a stretch of rock-strewn beach. Many of the wonderful aspects of Third Beach were there, but it seemed a completely new experience.

The lighting was grayer, and the colors more muted. Tide-dependent sea life clung all over the wave-crashed boulders. Sea stars, barnacles, anemones, gulls, cormorants, anchored plants, snails, clams. Some visiting people were thrown in as an afterthought. Wind rushed hard, carrying a tangible wave spray mist. The beach was half sand from the waves, and half rounded smooth stones cascading up to the landward slopes behind. I would have loved a wind-protected porch right there.

After letting Dad know I had experienced what I needed from the coast for this trip, we discussed possible plans and changed them several times. Eventual outcome: call in a reservation for a room and dinner at the Timberline Lodge by Mount Hood, and plow through any traffic towards Portland.

Too much traffic. Nothing much by east coast standards, but a flood by this trip's standards. We needed to get accustomed to it; we were heading east.

Dad did not want to push for a long distance, so we stopped at the Lamplighter Motel outside of Portland, off of 26. We piled our musty, festering laundry into the appropriate Laundromat machines. I watched some racing shows on TV while Dad watched the clothes. I came to relieve him of his watch, but he stayed while I picked out the evening's canned dinner delights from a supermarket.

ALL ABOUT A LITTLE LUXURY: TIMBERLINE LODGE AT MT HOOD

Day 24: 67 / 8518

This day was easy, ferry style. Even more relaxed and comfortable, actually. No cool, foggy winds to ice cube my head. Those winds were less than a foot from my elbow, but double panes made them untouchable. The Timberline Lodge's huge exposed wood beams, angular and simple in form, were providing cozy protection against the dense fog that was shot through with whipping snow.

The lack of mileage was reported to the No Complaint Department. We had originally intended to stick our noses into places around Mount Hood, wherever looked interesting for a view or hike. A soaking, chilling rain - that slushed into falling snow near the lodge – changed those plans. We quickly dismounted, with many quick-walking passers-by cracking friendly jokes about our wetness and motorcycles up there at snowy altitude.

The atmosphere of Timberline enveloped us immediately as we passed the carved wooden Indian head embedded in the entrance door. I was ready for a relaxing getaway spot like this, and Dad was ready to be pampered too.

The relaxation took hold of me: seduction into an afternoon nap and writing at a table littered with peanuts and glasses from the bar, all before dinner. The original, solid wood table got a good wiping with some left-over napkins, and I pulled up a hard but well butt-contoured chair. A family that spoke in a southern-draw joined me in the alcove of four tables, and I even became a stop on a packed lodge tour that provided the same information I heard earlier (and that the tour guide could likely repeat over and over backwards).

Dinner break: I treated Dad to a Father's Day meal, one of the best pile of vittles I ever had. The ambiance was great, with dark wood surrounds and fancy-pleasant service. Appetizer was stuffed mushrooms. I had never eaten mushrooms so tasty. The main course was even better. Poached salmon for Dad and Oregon pine-ridge salmon for me. All worth the extra wait and price, only to be topped by the best cheesecake I had ever slowly savored.

Snow starting to cover our bikes after arriving at Timberline Lodge

I returned later to my alcove. The noise became more intense, with loud laughing dinner parties and people sinking into a lodge version of nightlife. It included some of the strangest, most piercing laugh cackles ever heard. Hearing without seeing allowed me to pull the noise stampede apart and hear selected people and their attempts at civilized volume.

The snow was spraying down still, and the parking lot was getting lost in a dark, foggy swirl. Dad and I jumped outside to our bikes to see growing motorcycle snowdrifts. I hoped that the weather would clear for the next day and that all the snow removal equipment was ready to roll and shove. Otherwise, we were in for a long slide ride down the mountain road, or we could have been stranded. Not a bad oasis to be stranded in, but we were aiming home. Plus the lodge only had fashion magazines to read, so this could have been a Machiavellian problem of reading survival with stranded guests fighting over anything good in print.

The Timberline had a storied history, especially for a building. The Public Works Administration was convinced by vacationers and skiers to throw some of their anti-Depression money at carpenters and metalworkers to construct this huge, rough hewn place. Over fifteen months of hauling, pulleying, and forging, and 1.2 million dollars completed it. FDR officially dedicated the lodge in 1937.

I was impressed by the mammoth beams, animal-shape carved stair posts, solid rock walls, and massive smokestack chimneys. What a great idea, scaled down to size, for a house.

"What would this place probably cost to build nowadays?"

The ranger said, "We asked an architectural firm to estimate that on its 50th anniversary in 1987. The firm concluded it probably could not realistically be built in today's world of wages and materials, but a bill of 35 to 50 million dollars might do it."

Oh.

I outlasted the dinner din, but may not outlast the lodge.

PLACE FOR THOUGHT: COLUMBIA RIVER GORGE

Day 25: 551 / 9069

The journey had the feeling of winding down today, transitioning from going out to coming back. The off and on dashed road lines said so, as did the passing jumbles of sagebrush. Our direction east had a sense of home and the future beyond this journey. A sense of mileage guided us. It was time to watch and absorb some, and time to think.

The trip was definitely changing. We ate at a McDonald's this day. No more Bayshores. The towns had become regular American, connected by interstates of the usual car mix with the in-between slots filled by loaded trucks. The ground had been tread much more frequently before by millions of Goodyears.

The experience was not over yet, though, and it still threw valuable experiences at us. In fact, this morning opened up with great scenery continuing through Oregon. Timberline had been cozy, though the small end-framed bed contorted me for fit. Dad was still in a pamper-me mood, so the bellman was called to take our bags back to where we had hauled them from the day before, in the alcove by the Indian head.

We had to go out to our steeds and push off the covering snow. The bikes slowly and grudgingly started in the cold, and we needed to pull them out of their snow piles. The road down the mountain was surprisingly trouble free, only being wet and steaming from the bright sunlight warmly absorbing into exposed black asphalt.

Looking over our shoulders provided a bottom frame for Mount Hood, which we were truly seeing for the first time. A beautiful mountain, wind buffeted and deeply covered in shining snow. It rose up and steeper, ending in a huge near vertical rock block. Not just a cone or a mound, but instead a unique shape from lower to higher.

Mount Hood eventually disappeared for the last time around a corner, and we were heading east across Oregon country. The Columbia River Gorge opened up to say "aaaahhhhh", and I was swallowed. It was amazing country, completely unexpected and some of the most impressive scenery of the trip. And all this from an interstate on the cannonball trajectory back home!

Gusted from either side when we popped around a hill or over an open flat expanse, we weaved in our lane through the gorge. The wind, fortunately behind us for most of the day, was a Heaven-sent gift for the bright multi-colored windsurfers skimming over the Columbia's white caps. They criss-crossed each other's paths near shoreline take-off spots.

Rising to either side of them and us, ancient eroded canyons stood in segmented degrees of brown. Bare rock was shaped into hoodoos and rock slide walls. Hillsides were covered with dry grasses, short scrub, and stunted trees. And the overall effect was an amazing pass-through.

The area did not entice me in the same way as Denali or the Washington and Oregon coasts. The gorge was not intimate. It was an area where I planned to return, but not necessarily to get out and hike through for a finer, up close experience. Passing through on an open motorcycle seemed to fit this place. Without the changing perspectives and mind-overloading inputs, the impact may have been lessened. The river and bushes overshadowed an essentially barren, forbidding feel. An area to be oohed and aahed at, but not taken in or touched.

Oregon eventually ran out of its grand scale momentum, metamorphosizing into rolling hills of dusty, post-nuclear-war looking farmland. The interstate was in good, lower-48 shape, and the traffic matched the design of the road. Two lanes each way with moving traffic all over, and an eternal parade of transporting trucks.

Our gas up and go spot held us back from "going" when we decided to do dinner. We were at a place designed for trucks and truckers, and everyone else was considered extra money but unimportant. A sign in the restaurant warned that truckers would be served first over anyone else, so please be patient. Sure thing. Most likely a marketing strategy for making the truckers - this place's bread and butter - feel the king treatment.

Not that I had been in many truck stops, but the place seemed fancier and more modern than my preconceptions about truck stops. Very clean, well painted, with strong attempts to draw customers in, and funky bathrooms with showers and a public hair dryer. I had never seen much appeal in trucking as a profession, but this type of place probably served as a paradise interstate island for them.

Night crept up and then pounced. This was something that we had not been accustomed to for a while now. The sun would occasionally accompany us to bed up north, but the sun had long sunk below the dark horizon before we arrived at the Monterey Motor Inn in

Twin Falls, Idaho. What "Monterey" had to do with anything, I didn't know. Maybe some quaint, witty reason for the name. Maybe not.

The sun lowered itself below the haze, and the huge sky remained in light blue with pastel rainbow shades rimming the horizon. There was something special about the sky out there in the meek rolls of flatlands. It opened wide; huge to all horizons. Everything below looked smaller: Dad seemed a lit-up dot, and the trucks resembled kid-pushed toys. The mountains became hills. Railroads became N scale toys in a Christmas garden. And the sky just hovered and loomed.

PURE MOTION: ON TO COLORADO

Day 26: 522 / 9591

This day was pure travel, pure locomotion. We went through some great open spaces and it gave me a taste of Colorado, where roads twisted like a sine wave, covering the bottoms of valleys between mountains. I well remember a prior trip to the state, visiting my childhood friend Tom in Boulder. Rock-barricaded rivers flowed below and to a side, and the trees clung to soil filled with the remnants of other trees that slid long ago on top of slowly cascading rocks. The greens were deep, playing well against the reds and browns of the underlying soil and rock. And the non-shard hunks of rock were cracked by irregular lines and spaces, some looking ready to tumble while others were already pulled low by gravity.

The strange thing on this trip was that all of the "Colorado scenes" of memory were in Utah, and what I had previously envisioned as being in Utah was instead in Colorado. We had only traveled as far east as Craig, Colorado to the El Monte Inn, so the scenes combined with reality in other areas of the state.

In Boulder, my childhood friend Tom was there. I wanted to see him, especially with us being nearby, so I called his mother the day before to get all of the details. She only had his post office box number for location, which helped little in finding him, but she did have a phone number. Calling from a 7-11, pre-Slurpee, I asked him to guess who I was. Tom got it right on the first answer, and was glad I had called.

As usual, his situation was somewhat confusing. He apparently was working at wherever I first called him, but the dishwasher had been fired the week before at a separate place called Rudy's restaurant and he was needed as a replacement. There was some business connection between those two places and the seemingly cultish group I found him to be living and working with. When talking with his mother, she subtly slipped in her wish for me to "check out this place" and report back. The cultish tones of the ashram where he lived had probably worried her.

The letters he sent to me seemed happy with the deal, so it may have been good for him on some levels. I enjoyed hearing his voice again; it had been a long time. We left our phones with a plan: I would call Tom the next day at Rudy's when we got near or inside Boulder. End of plan.

That post-nuclear farmland gradually livened up. Long steel irrigation pipes on wheels rolled across crops, spraying green fertilized water. I even saw green hay bales for the first time. They were fresh cut and bundled, unlike the usual stacked dry-yellow. Extremes bounced around throughout the day, though. This farmland would disappear and reappear in new shapes, frequently after unusual, non-farmable land took up some of the Earthcrust we were rolling over. Some rows of crops contoured up a hill as steeply as practical, while other areas were flat to the horizon's mountains and had been rowed in circles to accommodate the pivoted rolling water irrigation systems. Straight lines and square plots still made their conventional appearances as well.

Extremes followed through a Grand Canyon-like scene, with its own twists. To my left were gorges formed by water both present and long gone, winding around the road and invisible around corners up into the hills. Tall, dark green trees followed the rivers and spread as far as the seeping water reached from the riverbanks. The rivers flowed over beds quietly, lit from inside like aquamarine in a ring. Immediately beyond the snaking river-dependent forest, everything quickly returned to brown-green grasses and several varieties of white-green bushes, all dry and hard.

To my right, the hills were like sand dunes of brown dirt and gray pieces of rock, all intertwined by the roots of stunted, half-living bushes.

After much distance of such passing scenes, our day ended with cranked-out miles and a more intimate feel from the land. Farms, communities, and ecosystems lived together. Still forbidding, but not as desolate.

HELPING A FRIEND

Day 27: 333 / 9924

The visit with Tom was a pleasant cap to a day of miles through beautiful Colorado scenes. Rocky Mountain National Park provided a high view looking down. Poopysuits protected us from the ascending cold, even keeping off the cool melt of occasional snow flurries. The road zagged across the faces of mountains, horizontal to clouds and vertical to sheer drops. The small town of Estes Park followed, descending into forest with views that looked up instead of down. Roads twisted out of the parks toward Nederland, where we met Tom in the parking lot of a local restaurant. We convoyed from there to the ashram.

A rocky, potholed dirt road led to the cabins, and we left our bags on the motorcycles for a beautiful hike along ex-horse riding trails to the summit of Rollins Peak. The trail required frequent stops to find out where we had just lost it, but sporadic rock cairns served as our progressive trail of breadcrumbs.

The summit was bare, pocked rock. Streams of gray rain were rippling down on distant mountains, and a river fitted its way through a valley below. Specks of cars could be seen on the road leading to the ashram, perpendicular over the train tracks which copied the shape of the river. Tom had slept up there one night in a warm breeze on pine needles and a sleeping bag. I understood why. Much was visible yet everything was distant enough to feel very removed. We haphazardly tried to follow gravity in a straight direction back, but course corrections were needed frequently. Two beds in a room full of more beds waited for us in the guest cabin. Dad read while Tom and I met in Tom's personal cabin.

I sat at Tom's desk. Rain was speckling the uninsulated roof with muffled crackling; the lack of insulation made for cold hands but soothing background sounds. His single room cabin on the grounds of the ashram was rustic and basic, but I could have easily enjoyed an out of the way cabin like his. He said he liked living simply, with poverty thrown into the recipe as a special ingredient.

The desk was utilitarian, like the rest of the room, and I dusted it off with the palms of my hands. The outside did not advertise electricity, but it was there. The dirty lit desk lamp concurred. The smell of just-boiled tea was subtly easing around its pot's edges, waiting and taunting since it had been left unattended. We would drink some later, after Tom came off of his bed and out of meditation.

Tom softly walked over to the pot and poured two mugs full, trying not to disturb me with the rattling spoon of his mixing honey. Tom sat cross-legged on his bed while I talked and walked around to different spots in the room, stopping for emphasis or wherever seemed comfortable. We discussed electricity being taken for granted, his ex-girlfriend Trish, and the graffiti left on the walls from when this was a girl's horse riding camp.

I shifted the subject to my prime area of concern for him: the commune-like meditation center that he was a believing part of. My first thoughts, when I read his vague descriptions in letters, centered around cults. His idealism and intelligence made him a susceptible candidate. "Checking it out", as his mother had wanted me to do, was always in my mind. No problem, I was planning on it anyhow.

Tom probably did not need someone else to mother him, but he genuinely appreciated my concern. After bringing it out openly and squarely, he thanked me. His hug the next morning said a lot. I initially picked up his books on the I Ching, an ancient Chinese philosophy that promoted inner peace and relied on mysticism. It was the basis for the teachings he received.

He respected my doubts of the mystical aspects. Random chance and heavily generalized statements worked like astrology: always right, with a wrong easily explained away. Whatever its faults though, Tom seemed to have mellowed and relaxed about life. His ex-girlfriend apparently "opened his eyes" to some problems at the ashram, and his unquestioning enthusiasm for the ashram had waned. But he felt it was a good experience for him, and in some ways I did as well. After talking with him about what were perhaps better paths ahead, he said he wanted to move out and away soon. He planned to restart college in the fall, majoring in environmental design. The experience at the ashram had put him on a personal track, and college seemed to be his next perceived crossing.

As to whether or not the ashram or the organization behind it had cultish aspects to it, I did not know enough about life there. Tom was free to move in and out as he desired, and the facilities were very pleasant and removed just enough from the road to be peaceful. It was officially a meditation center, but residents like Tom worked at an outside, connected job and did chores around the facilities. All for only room and board. In Tom's case, he worked as a dishwasher at Rudy's restaurant in Boulder, and had also been doing carpentry work on a new two story building to be used for administration and massage. That arrangement seemed lopsidedly in favor of the ashram, at least economically.

Trish apparently tuned him on to the organization's lack of conscientiousness and respect for the environment. He also recognized a use of fear and intimidation in some teachings and policies. Definite marks that made me wary. However, Tom seemed well and content, and his newfound see-through view of the organization was reassuring. Though he was not as critical or objective as I would have been, he was also a different person who might have rejected my level of cynicism. I hoped he would do well in his decisions ahead, and I had more confidence in that since I came to visit and talk it through with him.

Two weeks later, I received a letter from Tom. He had separated from the organization and was moving forward on his new path.

INSIDE THOUGHTS: CROSSING THE PLAINS

Day 28: 695 / 10619

We packed early the next morning to shove through miles. Tom bid farewell to us and our motorcycles, and we were gone bouncing and swerving along the ashram's driveway. I detuned my brain for the days ahead, paying little attention to my surroundings. Instead, I curled up inside my own thoughts, wandering aimlessly. The tactic was one of survival: give attention to traffic and set actions on autopilot so the long miles and hours would not make me go road bonkers. The plains opened up wide to us, and it was a very long day into the heart of the Midwest.

HARSH LESSONS, COMING HOME

Days 29-30: 1093 / 11712

The next day, to be considered our finale day of the trip, became the longest and most grueling ride of the entire journey. We fired up the engines at 10:20 Saturday morning, and occasionally swapped our bikes throughout the day. Our straight through mileage did not end until rolling over the home grass at 12:30 the next afternoon. If I learned from experience, I would learn this: never again ride over 24 hours straight and all through the night.

This masochistic plan was not a problem until around midnight. The lulling sensation of the motorcycle worked in synergy with my physical tiredness. The result was a Hellish chain of hours feeling miserable and trying hard to stay awake. I was not always successful, and later felt fortunate to be home unhurt. There were far too many nods of the head.

Then the dreaded event finally happened: I went to sleep while riding a motorcycle on a highway. The rough gravel of the road's edge woke me up. I said "Oh my God" to my helmet as I realized I was about to crash into a guardrail at full highway speed. A very fast counter-steer swerve, powered by instant-on adrenaline, let me get away with tucking my leg close to the gas tank and bouncing off the guardrail sideways with the projecting cylinders of the BMW's twin engine. The motorcycle wobbled and bucked violently, but I managed to stay upright.

My brain then told me I was moving back into traffic four lanes over from where I last enjoyed consciousness. I didn't know what was there and what I might run back into. A fast over-the-shoulder glance showed a blue car straddling the dashed lines, which was probably a result of avoiding the drifting, wobbling two wheeled maniac. A bug-eyed elderly couple stared at me in fright, incredulous at what just happened directly in front of them across the highway. The driving husband let off the gas completely and drifted back out of sight into the distance behind, never to be seen again. I wanted to wave an apology, but they just wanted to avoid me completely.

That certainly kept me awake until the next rest stop. Dad had not seen any of this since he was in front. After telling him about my acrobatic act, fatherly concern immediately took over. We were so close to home, I finally convinced him to continue on. He proposed different solutions which all worked to get me home: a nap at a 7-11, a cold water drenched towel around my neck, and gradually alternating movement of safe leapfrog positions as we cruised down the highway.

Quite a scary end to a great trip, but an educational experience nonetheless. The ramifications of my bold fighting against fatigue at different times during the journey finally caught up with me, convincing me to treat it with far more respect in the future. There were other journeys to be experienced.

EPILOGUE

Mom came bouncing happily out of the house, followed by my grinning brother Brian and our wagging dog Cedar. The stories began, starting generally and then honing in on the fondest vignettes. Unpacking the bags would wait.

Time left on our journey dwindled to a point and receded away. The trip was over, but there was so much to remember and many thoughts to play with, expanding on them for the future. I was ready for a vacation from vacation, but I knew I would want to be back out there again very soon. Most likely too soon.

The journey opened up the world to me. It emphasized independence and "just making it come together" to accomplish a goal and an adventure. I saw so much, met so many people, and experienced so many new things, and yet this was just a small vignette within the world's story.

It reinforced and ingrained so many high values for me, serving as guideposts for the future. Dad would have quit his job if his employer hadn't given him the month off to fulfill his promise, and he made sure it all occurred through a determination and purpose that was inspiring. Mom and Dad had achieved getting me all the way through college. They supported me, my education, and my life to whatever highest level I wanted to achieve. And we celebrated with something far more meaningful than any graduation present I had ever heard from anyone else. It was all about family and being mutually involved in all of this, all together. We weren't constrained by norms, but instead achieved our goals.

It was post-college and my first real job was about to begin. The stage of life beyond home was upon me. This journey was my bridge.

Thank you Dad, for having the vision and integrity to see our 10 year journey through, and sincerely fulfilling a grand promise. And thank you Mom, for being the supportive and caring home base for all our wacky ideas.

ABOUT THE AUTHOR

Scott lives in Seattle with his wife Karen (who is from Portland). They both enjoy traveling and sharing their experiences with others. Twenty years later in 2009, his parents moved to Whidbey Island in Washington state. The journey in this book changed all of their lives much more than they would have ever known back in 1989. For more information, please visit www.CelebrateBig.com.

To Order Additional Copies of

FROM MARYLAND TO ALASKA AND BACK: A PROMISE FULFILLED

visit us online at

www.CelebrateBig.com/promise

Or Ask Your Local Bookseller

www.ingramcontent.com/pod-product-compliance
Lightning Source LLC
LaVergne TN
LVHW011232080426
835509LV00005B/457